Telling Time

Telling Time

Sketch of a Phenomenological Chrono-logy

FRANÇOISE DASTUR

translated by Edward Bullard

THE ATHLONE PRESS
LONDON & NEW BRUNSWICK, NJ

First published in the United Kingdom 2000 by
THE ATHLONE PRESS
1 Park Drive, London NW11 7SG
and New Brunswick, New Jersey

Publisher's Note
The publishers wish to record their thanks to the French Ministry of Culture for a grant towards the cost of translation.

British Library Cataloguing in Publication Data
A catalogue record of this book is available from the British Library

ISBN 0 485 11520 4

Library of Congress Cataloging-in-Publication Data
Dastur, Françoise, 1942–
[Dire le temps. English]
Telling time: sketch of a phenomenological chrono-logy / Françoise Dastur: translated by Edward Bullard.
p. cm.
Includes bibliographical references and index.
ISBN 0-485-11520-4 (alk. paper)
1. Time. 2. Phenomenology. 3. Heidegger, Martin, --1889–1976.
I. Title.
BD638.D35413 2000
115--dc21 99-36615
CIP

Distributed in the United States, Canada and South America by
Transaction Publishers
390 Campus Drive
Somerset, New Jersey 08873

Typeset by Columns Design Limited, Reading
Printed and bound in Great Britain by
Cambridge University Press

To the memory of
Alexandre, Anna and Fernand.

Contents

Contents

By way of an epigraph, allow me to quote from Félix Ravaisson's 'Dessin' in *Dictionnaire de Pédagogie* (Ferdinand Buisson, 1882) this sentence, apt also for the art of writing, from the author of *De l'habitude*, a work in which I have always seen the very model of the thesis:

> *The secret of the art of drawing is to discover in each object the particular manner in which a certain flexuous line, its generative axis as it were, advances across its length and breadth like a wave breaking up into ripples.*

and this remark of Heidegger's reported by Roger Munier, in *Stèle pour Heidegger* (Paris: Arfuyen, 1992), p. 17:

> *Then when I ask Heidegger what language will ever be capable of expressing this ecstatic Denken:*
>
> *– A very simple language, he replies. Eine ganz einfache Sprache, whose rigour will consist less in the verbiage (Gerede) of an apparent technicity than in the absolute nakedness of expression. And Heidegger adds with a smile:*
>
> *- In the future, philosophical books will no longer be very large books . . .*

Author's Note

The following text reproduces without significant alterations (with the exception of the epilogue, added subsequently) the principal argument of a thesis submitted at the University of Louvain (Belgium) in June 1993.

To clarify the context of this argument, it seemed useful to add as an appendix the paper read at the time of the submission of the thesis.

Prologue

'*Wir kommen nie zu Gedanken. Sie kommen zu uns.*' 'We never come to thoughts. They come to us,' wrote Heidegger in one of the pages bearing witness to the experience of thinking, brought together in a work of his significantly entitled ***Aus** der Erfahrung des Denkens*, '*From* the Experience of Thinking'.

It is the *coming* in its pure nakedness, not the coming of something or of someone, but the coming *itself* and its inapparent event, which will be in question here.

That what comes in the coming is always the *clearing* [*éclaircie*] of a thought that can provide, for beings capable of death, the space of a habitable *clearing* [*clairière*], this is something that did not await the birth of philosophy to be *told* in myth or poem.

For thought, as Heidegger recalls at the beginning of the "Letter on Humanism", is, in the double sense of the genitive, thought of the *verbum infinitivum* that is in the grammar of our languages the word "to be" [*être*]. It is the gift that comes from being and is *at the same time* taking care of it and giving the response which is its due.

But how can the very *event* of thought be thought, this *simultaneity* in which two movements of opposite

direction are one? How can the *flash of lightning* which at once unites and disjoints world and thought be told?

That synthesis is always also diaeresis, that gathering is at the same time separation, however, is what is said without becoming apparent in the double phonetic and semantic articulation of every *saying*.[tn]

For this flash is *the very event of language*, which does not mean that human beings are anachronically the measure of all things but, on the contrary, that there is no assignable origin of the dialogue that immemorially *we* are.

Ψυχης εστι λογος εαυτον αυξων:[1] it is proper to breathe to be a λογος that increases of itself, Heraclitus says, and elsewhere adds that it is the depth of this λογος, regarded by him as inseparable from the vastness [*vastité*] of the world, which renders the limits of breath unlocatable.[2] Aristotle also understands ψυχη as an επιδοσις εις αυτο,[3] a growth into itself, thus granting to what he elsewhere names φωνη σεμαν–τικη[4] (a meaningful sound) an internal transcendence wresting it from the start out of the immanence of self-presence. This is the foundation of the intrinsic historicity of speech, which, through a process of conservation that is at the same time an overcoming, renders speech, like history, the knowledge and the result of itself and not the monotonous iteration of the identical.

This internal dialectic of language, which always speaks at the same time of something else and of itself

and which is related to the structural inter-subjectivity of discourse, is that of an *originary spontaneity* which takes on its full sense only when thought on the basis of mortality. For it is and it is not our own, it precedes us whilst coming to pass only in us in a difference that is also homology. And, above all, it "produces" only the "*nihil originarium*"[5] of the world. It creates therefore, according to the διακοσμος εοικοτα[6] that Parmenides already saw coming to pass in naming, only this jewel of nothing for which death is the casket.

Glossary

The original thesis used, and this translation retains, a number of foreign words taken from Greek and German. This short glossary is merely a guide to the meanings of the principal terms so used.

λογος	statement, account, reason
λεγειν	saying
Ereignis	event of appropriation
Gegnet	region, open domain in which a being can be encountered, free expanse
Gespräch	dialogue, conversation

In addition, an original French term has on occasion been quoted by the translator in square brackets following its English translation.

1

The Idea of a Phenomenological Chrono-logy

> *Judgement* is our oldest belief, our most habitual holding-true or holding-untrue.... If I say: 'lightning flashes' I have posited the flash once as an activity and a second time as a subject: I have thus presupposed a being underlying the event, a being that is not identical to the event but rather *remains*, *is*, and does not '*become*'.[1] (Nietzsche)

Can we tell time? This question might initially seem pointless, if we consider that every language, and *a fortiori* the languages of the Indo-European family, whose morphology rests on the distinction between noun and verb and which are characterised by the development of verbal forms, is given not as a simple 'semiotic' practice that would establish the inventory of already given 'objects' but as an 'activity' of the articulation of the presence in the world of a 'subject' who can be separated from it only 'in the imagination'.[2]

Yet the question of the temporality of discourse has not ceased to haunt secretly the entire Western philosophical tradition that can be said to have been born of the reflection of the Greek thinkers upon their

idiom. Without undertaking here an inventory of the steps that led to the 'nominalist' ontology of the Platonic theory of ideas, we must nevertheless briefly recall the part played by the 'grammatical'[3] awakening in the elaboration of the mode of thought termed 'philosophy' in Greece. Bruno Snell, in his collection of 'studies devoted to the birth of European philosophy', entitled *Die Entdeckung des Geistes* (*The Discovery of the Mind*), notes the decisive character of the transformation of the demonstrative pronoun into the definite article for the formation of philosophical thought and emphasises Cicero's difficulty in translating the Platonic idea into a language which lacked it.[4] But one must also recall the accent placed in the genesis of philosophical thought, from the singularity of the Parmenidian εον (being) to the Platonic μετεξις (participation), on the nominal and verbal mode of the participle.[5] For this grammatical 'category', which attained the highest point of its development in the Greek language, is the origin of the duality of sense, simultaneously existential and categorial, of the concept of being. It is this combination of essential-being and accidental-being that one finds hypostasised in the το ον (being) studied by Aristotelian πρωτη φιλοσοφια (First Philosophy), and it was the source of the dual 'ontological' and theological problem posed by Aristotle in response to the question τι το ον ("What is being?") and of the fundamental structure that the Middle Ages would call 'metaphysics'.

These two examples show the importance lent to

naming and to the noun in the development of conceptual thought. As has often been remarked, the Platonic question of essence coincides with that of the noun, and it is precisely because of this privilege accorded to the noun over the verb that philosophy was to be drawn from the beginning to orient itself towards the search for separate forms.[6] If the Aristotelian response to the Platonic χωρισμος (separation) consists in showing that 'being is said in several ways' and that it is therefore not exterior to our 'interpretation', this does not mean that the analysis of language undertaken under the title Περι ερμηνειας (*On Interpretation*) makes the verb the centre of the proposition.[7] On the contrary, for Aristotle 'the verb (ρεμα) is always the sign (σημειον) of what is said of *another* thing, knowledge of things belonging to a subject (υποκειμενον) or contained in a subject',[8] which implies that the verb itself is only a predicate and that the noun (ονομα) is the support of the intentional relation with the object. This is why the verb, taken in isolation outside the proposition (λογος) which alone is meaningful, is in reality a noun,[9] even though, contrary to the noun, which is 'without reference to time',[10] it adds to its own meaning that of time.[11] It is significant here that this προσσεμαινον χρονον, reference to time, does not come to be identified with the πτωσις ρηματος, the grammatical tense of the verb, but signifies the present assumption of the proposition by the speaker. Now, this happens only at the *synthetic* level of the proposition as the definition of the

negative expression as αοριστον ρημα, indefinite verb, attests.[12] Thus, we can clearly see here the definition of noun and verb as purely logical forms whose interlacing alone constitutes the λογος independently of their relation to 'real' temporality.[13]

The relation to time, however, is effectively inscribed in the very syntax of Greek which, being Indo-European, is an inflected language.[14] Moreover, this is how it understood itself in the treatise on the analysis of linguistic expression: Περι ερμηνειας (*On Interpretation*). Aristotle employs the same term πτωσις to designate the declension of the noun as for the declension of the verb,[15] and this word, from the verb πιπτω, "to fall", was to be translated by the Latin *casus* and reserved by the grammarians of the Hellenistic epoch for the declension of the substantive alone, whilst the word εγκλισις, which means 'inclining', served to designate the inflections of the modalities of the verb. In the section of *An Introduction to Metaphysics* devoted to 'The grammar of the word "being"' Heidegger remarks that the choice of these terms was due to the fact that the Greeks understood being on the basis of a being stood up, remaining standing and so freely achieving a stable installation in the necessity of its limit. It is what holds itself in this way, in itself, from its limit, and thus offers itself to the look which they termed ειδος or ιδεα, on the basis of an unquestioned (*fraglos*) identification of being with parousia or presence.[16] From this we understand that Aristotle designates proposi-

tions in the past tense, as well as those in the future, as πτωσεις ρηματος, as tenses of verbs, because in both cases non-presence finds itself related to the form of realised and stable presence on which it has merely an 'oblique', retrospective or anticipatory view. The 'form' of presence thus finds itself preserved in a *privative* manner in the very midst of temporality.[17]

What we are engaged with here is thus, on the one hand, the birth of the logical form of judgement understood as the synthesis of concepts and, on the other, the implicit understanding of discourse as the presentation of being [*l'étant*]. What characterises Aristotle's thought is precisely that the importance he attributes to logical synthesis diverts his attention, so to speak, from the properly 'disclosive' character of discourse, yet without the latter having already been reduced to the status of the pure and simple 'proposition'. It is this singular position of Aristotle's which is analysed at length by Heidegger in his course of 1925–6 entitled *Logik. Die Frage nach der Wahrheit* ("Logic. The Question of Truth"). Heidegger's task at this period, which saw the completion of *Being and Time*, is to account for the a-temporal character of logical truth, which Husserl had defined as identity and 'validity' – representing in this respect the culmination of the whole logical tradition – through an interrogation of its historical foundations. What emerges from the analysis to which he submits the Aristotelian definition of the λογος αποφαντικος (apophantic) is that the determining and synthesising character of the

logical proposition, though founded upon exhibition or presentation (*Aufweisung*) constitutive of the primary function of the λογος, can nevertheless be detached from it and present itself as a pure relation between two concepts or a formal synthesis.[18] Now, what characterises Aristotle's position is that he recognises the apophantic character of the λογος, uncovering and showing, in synthesis only, and it is the latter that constitutes for him the structural sense of the λογος in general. To the extent that this synthesis is taken as merely formal synthesis, the possibility of understanding what meaning, understanding, interpretation and ultimately language itself are is foreclosed.[19] However, in contrast, the founder of propositional logic himself in no way viewed the λογος as a judgement, i.e., the connection of mental representations understood as 'images' of things, but saw it as a pure αποφανσις that makes (or 'lets') the being itself appear. For synthesis is for Aristotle not solely a structure of the λογος, but also a structure of beings themselves, as several passages of the *Metaphysics* testify.[20]

As a Greek, Aristotle could grasp the phenomena only through language and so was unable to distinguish the apophantic level of the proposition from the properly existential level termed hermeneutic by Heidegger.[21] In the interpretation of his position given by Heidegger at this period, what is to be shown is that even if Aristotle did not explicitly understand truth otherwise than as the correspondence between two sub-

sisting beings – the proposition on the one hand and the thing on the other, if he was unable to perceive it as a relation of an existence to a world, as the *Weltoffenheit* of a Dasein, nevertheless he was able to hold firm to the phenomena themselves without obliterating them through the construction of a 'picture' theory of truth.[22] This is why it is important to insist on the significance of those passages of the *Metaphysics* where it becomes apparent that it is beings themselves and not propositions about them which are understood as 'synthetic'. The concept of συνθεσις (synthesis) consequently turns out to be both a logical and an ontological one, or perhaps, as Heidegger suggests, one which can be located in neither one domain nor the other since it has the 'function' of uniting them. This non-separation of the logical and ontological characterises the Aristotelian phase of philosophy just as it does Platonic philosophy. For, according to Heidegger, it is one of Plato's immortal merits to have acknowledged, *contra* Parmenides, the being of error and falsity[23] and so to have allowed Aristotle to show that falsity, like truth, belongs to beings themselves and not simply to thought. Through the analysis of chapter 10 of the *Metaphysics*, book Θ, Heidegger shows that, for Aristotle, synthesis is a condition of falsity, not solely as the structure of the λογος, but as the structure of beings themselves.[24] If the apprehension of simple beings (ασυνθετα) presents no possibility of falsity but simply the ignorance (αγνοια)[25] that is the failure to grasp, grasping (θιγειν) itself being what defines truth at

this level, then this implies that complex beings only can be objects of error and give rise to false propositions. Therefore, for error to be possible there must be synthesis *both* in the being itself and in the related proposition. But this relation itself, of 'ontological' and 'logical' synthesis, rests on the identification of being and truth such as Aristotle postulated it at the level of simple beings where θιγειν defines αληθες and where a comportment – grasping – defines the being of simple beings. Thus truth can no longer be located solely at the level of the proposition, rather, as Heidegger affirms with vigour, it makes the proposition itself possible.[26]

*

However, what remains unquestioned in the Aristotelian theory of ontological truth is the properly *temporal* sense of the identification of being and presence. This is what leads Heidegger to 'The Idea of a Phenomenological Chronology'.[27] Its task is to investigate the temporality of phenomena, by which must be understood not their being in time, which still remains an extrinsic determination, but what in their very structure is characterised by time.[28] This investigation of temporality and of time itself has, of course, nothing to do with the historical discipline of the same name and represents, on the contrary, a fundamental philosophical inquiry. Connecting it with the other disciplines of philosophical science, or even sketching the outline of a new systematicity of them in relation

to it, however, is not Heidegger's task as 'it could be that the entrenchment of these traditional disciplines finds itself shaken by this chronology and that, on the basis of it, it might be completely senseless to propose a classification in the traditional sense'.[29] This is why all that counts here is to determine the task incumbent upon this chronology, whose domain is as yet undelimited, as is attested by the uncertainty reigning over the philosophical use of determinations of time and the crude manner with which one customarily opposes the temporal to the a-temporal, as if this were the simplest thing in the world.

Heidegger was nevertheless not absolutely without predecessors in this enterprise. Kant was for him 'the only one to have advanced into this obscure domain, without however coming to perceive the principal meaning of his attempt'.[30] It was in the Kantian theory of the schematism that Heidegger saw an essential approach to the chronological problem, namely the exposition of the temporality of those comportments of Dasein that are, in Kantian terms, transcendental apperception, acts of understanding and consciousness taken in the broadest sense.[31] The whole of the final part of the course of 1925–6 (comprising over a third of it) was to be devoted to an initial interpretation of the role played by time in the Transcendental Aesthetic and Analytic of the *Critique of Pure Reason*. Heidegger did not consider, in the Hegelian manner, that the relationship between the schematism of the understanding and sensibility remains 'exterior' and

so not 'dialectical' enough. Rather, in the face of the difficulty of this analysis of the secret judgements of the common reason in which philosophy consists,[32] he sought to retain the attitude of restraint before the phenomena adopted by Kant and so to advance, in his wake, into the night of the soul and its 'hidden art' without attempting hastily to master and subject to the violence of the concept (as does Hegel in his 'imposing system') the problems prudently left unresolved by Kant.[33]

The project of a 'phenomenological chronology' is therefore inscribed, in the manner of a kind of regulative ideal, in the enterprise which Heidegger assigned himself of a radicalisation of the problem of traditional logic which is to be, at once, revived and shaken by being referred back to its philosophical source.[34] If Heidegger firmly takes the side of the development of a 'philosophising logic' against the teaching of traditional school logic, he does so in the *phenomenological* sense of the injunction of the return to the things themselves and of the questioning back from the sedimentation resulting from history. For him 'traditional school logic is the exteriorised, deracinated and therefore rigidified content of an originary philosophical questioning which was alive in Plato and Aristotle, a questioning which was completely suffocated by the ossification proper to the school exercises'[35] and its teaching, far from sharpening and disciplining thought, can even lead, when it becomes 'pure rote learning and blind erudition', to 'an empty quibbling' and 'wran-

gling'.[36] It is hopeless to expect a training in thinking from traditional logic, for even as scientific thought it 'can be learnt only in dealings with things'.[37] The challenge to traditional logic is nevertheless perfectly reconcilable with a true respect for the tradition; it consists not in a blind attachment to and the stubborn reproduction of the past, but rather in 'the philosophical appropriation of the authentic philosophical content which it holds'.[38]

So, what Heidegger is aiming at is 'transparency' in scientific research, which can be obtained only if it first understands itself as a form of existence and agrees to put the question 'What is truth?' explicitly. This involves having the courage not simply to confront the possibility of error but also to admit it. For this aspiration to the transparency of Dasein with respect to itself must in no way be confused with the desire for the plenitude of a self-presence delivered from all mediation. It must, on the contrary, be understood as 'the courage of the interior liberation with respect to one's own self [*des Eigenen Selbst*] in the ability to listen and to learn, the courage of positive explication (with others) [*Auseinandersetzung*]'.[39] Thus, in affirming that such a transparency is possible only by way of a philosophising logic, Heidegger suggests the necessarily intersubjective character, not simply of philosophical questioning itself, but also of the 'thing' of which it treats, which, being inseparable from the historicality of language, can in no way be assimilated to a pre-given objectivity. The 'de-temporalisation' at

the origin of the 'formal' character of traditional logic also entails the 'naturalisation' of the 'object' and 'contents' of thought, which, however, are 'nothing' outside of their 'grammatical clothing'.[40]

*

There is no trace of this projected 'phenomenological chronology' either in *Being and Time* or, it would appear, in the Marburg or Freiburg courses published to date, which precede the time of the 'turn'. Following the latter, the perspective of the development of a 'temporal ontology' will be abandoned and with it the idea that the temporal horizon could suffice to account for what we term being. In this way, Heidegger turns towards a thought of the *Gegnet* and of the unity of the *Zeitraum* (space-time) to attain access to what alone constitutes the openness of the domain of the manifestation of beings.[41] For, if what is termed 'being' in *Being and Time* is nothing other than time,[42] after the *Kehre* (turn) it is not so much a question of thinking on the basis of space what is given increasingly as the 'exteriority' of being in relation to a Dasein understood less and less as subjectivity, as it is a question of dissociating time itself from its complicity with 'inner' sense. It is no longer a question of referring spatiality to temporality but rather of thinking the spacing of time itself. Heidegger attempted this from the *Beiträge zur Philosophie* (*Contributions to Philosophy*) on, in forging the expression *Zeitraum*[43]

designating (as is apparent in the seminar "Time and Space" of 1962) not the 'space-time' of physicists but rather the clearing opened by giving at a distance – the reciprocal *Reichen* (giving to one another) of the future, the having-been and the present – on whose basis alone what we term space becomes comprehensible.[44] This is why, when Heidegger emphasises that the question of the meaning of being, after having become that of the truth of being at the moment of the *Kehre*, finally took the form of the question of the place or locality of being,[45] one must not see in this last formulation of the 'topology of being' a denial of the previous project of a 'chronology' but on the contrary its re-actualisation, time now no longer being determined in a still metaphysical (which means transcendental) way as the foundation of being but as deploying the 'space' of a habitation.

If Heidegger had thus, for his part, abandoned the term 'chronology', just as he had indeed 'phenomenology',[46] without, however, entirely refusing to hint at a programme with the new designation 'topology of being', this does not mean that the task designated by these rubrics had been judged unaccomplishable but that the mode of its accomplishment could no longer be that of the λογος in its traditional sense. For, what is really worthy of question in this 'rubric' of chronology, which I propose to take up again here, is not so much the reference to time as the reference to logic it entails. Is it therefore possible to take up the project of a philosophising logic that was Heidegger's at the time

of *Being and Time*? Can one envisage the constitution of a new logic able to reintegrate into its 'propositions' the temporal moment exiled in the constitution of the scientific object, and which could give its rightful place to what Gadamer calls 'the inner historicity of experience'?[47] It is clear that when Heidegger talks of a 'topology' he no longer understands the λογος, still at issue here, in the traditional manner. The expression 'topology of being' is seen for the first time in a not very scientific-looking text entitled precisely 'The Experience of Thinking' and in a context where what is at issue is as much the still veiled poetic character of thinking as it is a thinking poetry. Moreover, it is the latter that is 'in truth the topology of being' and tells being 'the site where it deploys itself'.[48] The λογος to which Heidegger refers here is considered no longer in its semantic-epistemic aspect only but also in the syntactic and poetic aspect that equally belongs to it and that permits him to see in thought not only an essential preliminary of action but 'action [. . . that is] the simplest and at the same time the highest', as the first page of the 'Letter on Humanism' affirms.[49] At the end of a text devoted to Heraclitus and to the more originary essence of a λογος in which the Greeks dwelled, but without ever having thought it, Heidegger declares that 'thought transforms the world' by rendering it more enigmatic, more obscure and more profound, by tearing it from its pure and simple presence to bring it into the 'storm of being'.[50]

But does not the 'lightning flash' character of such a

λογος consequently forbid any programmatic presentation of what could still present itself as a positive, even if non-epistemic, discipline under the name of chrono-logy? And should we not rather abandon that which could not fail to present itself as an enterprise of a more originary refounding of traditional logic and abandon the still traditional form that such an enterprise would necessarily take? Were such a position to be adopted, however, this abandonment could not be silent and would doubtless require extensive argumentation.[51] However, another course will be followed here. Not the programmatic presentation, in a negative sense, of an impossible discipline, but the *sketch* of what could, in a novel sense, be a 'logic' of temporality. For such a chronology does not permit programming or projecting in a transcendental sense, in no way does it consist in the inscription of determined limits. It is, on the contrary, destined in its essence to the unfulfilment and the inchoativity that Merleau-Ponty recognised as inevitable for the 'movement', rather than doctrine or system, that was phenomenology.[52] This is why, as with the latter, only a sketch [*l'esquisse*] is appropriate, which is to say, in its literal sense, improvisation.[53] Improvising is letting time 'happen', trusting the favour of the 'moment', but also facing the unexpected and the risk of failure.

The task at hand is therefore to draw such a sketch lightly, with the haste characteristic of all the enterprises of the mortals that humans are, and with a negligence applied to preserving the suppleness of the

ephemeral constructions that will shelter for a time (that of the 'thesis') the movement that, ceaselessly being reborn from its own interruptions, we call life or thought.

It is true that 'precipitation' has been strongly criticised in modern philosophy, inasmuch as the latter understands itself as an enterprise of foundation. Kant makes this point well in the introduction to the *Critique of Pure Reason*:[54] 'It is, indeed, the common fate of human reason to complete its speculative structures (*Gebaüde*) as speedily as may be, and only afterwards to inquire whether the foundations (*Grund*) are reliable.' The 'methodological' and 'architectonic' concerns become, in effect, one with the philosophical enterprise itself, which, as an eminently 'logical' enterprise, requires that 'patience of the concept' which finds its finest illustration in Hegelian discourse as absolute discourse. Haste and precipitation, like unfinished and weak constructions, are, on the contrary, rather the fate of a finite thought, which, because it is ceaselessly wending its way, must content itself with ephemeral shelter and, as the poet says, can truly dwell only in the lightning flash.[55]

2

Phenomenology and Temporality

> During the time that a motion is being perceived, a grasping-as-now takes place moment by moment; and in this grasping, the actually present phase of the motion itself becomes constituted. But this now apprehension is, as it were, the head attached to the comet's tail of retentions relating to the earlier now-points of the motion.[1] (Husserl)

In what sense, however, is the chrono-logy now to be sketched 'phenomenological'? In the course given in the winter semester of 1925–6 Heidegger specifies in this regard: 'In adding the adjective "phenomenological" to chronology, we want to indicate that this logos of time, this investigation of time has a philosophical orientation and has nothing whatever to do with the order of succession and the science of establishing dates.'[2] Therefore, 'phenomenological' here has the sense of 'philosophical' in contrast to the 'positive' character of the science called 'chronology'. In this, Heidegger is in perfect agreement with Husserl who constantly emphasised the fact that the term 'phenomenology' designates 'a method and an attitude of thought: the specifically *philosophical attitude of*

thought and the specifically *philosophical method*' and who affirmed that philosophy situates itself 'in a *totally new dimension*' relative to any natural knowledge and thus relative to any positive science.[3] It is with Husserl that the term 'phenomenology' becomes the very name of philosophy, as moreover he explicitly recognised in that manifesto of phenomenology that is the 'Epilogue' to his *Ideas* where it is emphasised that 'phenomenological science', 'the science of a new beginning', is in reality the restitution of 'the most original idea of philosophy' which found its first coherent expression with Plato and is the basis of European philosophy and science.[4] This is the idea of a 'universal science' and of a 'rigorous science' that is its own final justification and could find only a temporary and relative realisation in an historical process that is itself endless.[5] Nevertheless, it remains to be explained why the term 'phenomenology' became the very name of philosophy only in a recent phase of a long history, which has been dominated, since Plato, by the opposition between being and appearance and, since Aristotle's *Metaphysics,* by the question of being *qua* being. The term 'phenomenology' appeared for the first time in 1764 in Johann Heinrich Lambert's *Neues Organon* in which it was defined as the science of appearances, but one must await the year 1806 to see the term come to occupy a pre-eminent position in the philosophical scene. Hegel had at first given the title 'Science of the Experience of Consciousness' to the work he was in the process of completing, but during its actual publication renamed it 'Phenomenology of

Spirit'. However, it was nearly a century later, in 1901, in the second volume of Husserl's *Logical Investigations*, entitled 'Investigations in Phenomenology and the Theory of Knowledge', that phenomenology definitively left behind the subordinate status and the role of propaedeutic science, which it had until then been assigned, to take on the 'modern' name of philosophy.

Philosophy, as an autonomous mode of thought,[6] could have been born only of the withdrawal of the divine – to which Sophocles's tragedies testify – that followed the decay of the Greek political world: it is because the microcosm was no longer the image of the macrocosm that the boundary between the divine and the human became an enigma and the meaning of 'being' became aporetic.[7] With Aristotle philosophy determined itself as the 'precise science' that would later, with Clauberg and Wolff, be called ontology.[8] However, as Nietzsche vigorously emphasised in *On the Genealogy of Morals*, philosophy would have to cast off the priestly robes under which it had hidden and cease to confuse itself, in its movement of 'evasive transcendence'[9] and in its promotion of the aesthetic ideal, with theology, in order to become truly itself, which involves access to the true freedom of the will.[10] This is what was already coming to pass, whatever Nietzsche might say, when Kant turned his back on the traditional solution of making human beings participate in divine understanding: with Kant philosophy has to become atheistic.[11] That is to say, it has to begin with the *intuitus derivativus* of the finite being,

implying that the science of the phenomenal, the phenomenology of which Lambert spoke, no longer is a simple negative propaedeutic to metaphysics but is an essential moment of its elaboration. What was to be constituted in 1781 was, in effect, an ontology of the thing as phenomenon, for the knowledge of the phenomenal was no longer that of an appearance but of the thing such as it is for a non-productive intuition in opposition to the thing in itself, which is the correlate of an *intuitus originarius*. Nevertheless, phenomenology became the effective title only of a philosophy that had exchanged its overly modest name for that of science with Hegel, who thinks appearance as a trait of being itself. None the less, it remains the case that here also phenomenology constitutes, at best, a first division of science – that of the knowledge of appearance in which the opposition between being and appearance persists – while metaphysics proper, *The Science of Logic*, is possible only from the point of view of absolute knowledge, of the identity of object and subject, of thinking and thought, of appearance and being. For phenomenology to become, not merely the negative, but the *positive* name of philosophy, Husserl would have to break with Kantian noumenology just as much as with Hegelian absolute science. Phenomenological consciousness could no longer be thought of as the representational consciousness of an in-itself that would pre-exist it but as consciousness constituting the meaning of all being for us – and there is no being other than being for us. Husserl thus refuses the Kantian

distinction between two modes of intuition, not to assume the point of view of God in the Hegelian fashion, but on the contrary to generalise the *intuitus derivativus*[12] and attribute it to God himself, the only way of not positing a being behind the phenomenon. For Husserl, there are only interpreted beings, and it is in this way that he doubtless joins Nietzsche in his critique of the in-itself.[13]

*

However, since the discovery of the phenomenological reduction,[14] Husserlian phenomenology has borne a transcendental countenance and the declared sense of an idealism.[15] But, as well as not confusing idealism with the theory of the duality of worlds – whose genesis and decline Nietzsche recounts in the *Twilight of the Idols*, a theory which the philosophers who have been mentioned in the course of this 'history of an error' have all strongly criticised[16] – one must emphasise the very particular character of phenomenological idealism, which, as Husserl emphasises, is transcendental idealism in a fundamentally novel sense since, being nothing other than the laying out of the ego, it can do without the limit concept of the thing in itself. Never has the aspiration to the ideal taken the form of a true positivism[17] more decisively than in Husserl's thought; with an explicitly anti-Copernican[18] move, he seeks to *found* the ideal on the real, and the categorial on the sensible, thus confirming Heraclitus's affirmation according to

which 'the upward and downward paths are one and the same'.[19] The founded act comprising categorial intuition demands that receptivity and spontaneity are no longer opposed to one another but are instead in a relation of reciprocal conditioning and implication, as a sensible intuition must found the categorial élan, but, *at the same time*, this primary receptivity must, in some way, be 'neutralised' by the spontaneity of the idea that for its part makes sensible perception itself possible. In effect, categorial acts, as founded acts, reveal in a new way only what is already given at the level of 'simple' perception, whether they are acts of synthesis making explicit the sensible given according to its categorical moments, and thus allowing it to be expressed in propositions, or acts of ideation constituting new ideal objectivities on the basis of sensible perception. Though it is true that singular perception, which serves as a foundation for eidetic intuition, does not constitute the content of the idea in the case of ideation, while in a synthetic act it is taken up as the content of the new ideal objectivity, it is no less true that the act of categorial ideation must also found itself in a singular perception, which it neutralises.[20] Heidegger, in the interpretation given during the summer semester of 1925 in his course on the fundamental discoveries of phenomenology, amongst which he counts categorial intuition besides intentionality and the original sense of the a priori, places emphasis upon the thesis of the foundation of the categorial in the sensible and sees in it a new formulation of the

Aristotelian proposition from *De Anima* [21] according to which 'the soul never thinks without an image',[22] the image taking the place of sensation, as Husserl himself explicitly recognised.[23] This bringing together of Husserl and Aristotle, which is certainly not totally arbitrary, aims to demonstrate the absurdity of an intellect thought of as independent of sensibility in a broad sense, which is to say of a *given* that shows itself in its perceptive presence or in its imaginative re-presence and that aims at discrediting 'the old mythology'[24] of a pure intellect and of a form independent of matter, at the origin of the 'formal' character attributed to logic, and which has, since Boethius, spawned the quarrel over Universals and given birth to nominalism. With the discovery of categorial intuition, itself made possible only by the discovery of intentionality, Husserl reopened the way to ontology and gave it the scientific method of an inquiry that remains within phenomenality itself, since: 'There is no ontology *alongside* a phenomenology. Rather, *scientific ontology is nothing but phenomenology*.'[25]

Thus we can say of Husserlian idealism what we are already in a position to affirm of Kantian idealism: namely, that it consists in reopening at the level of the sensible itself the difference open since the birth of philosophy between the sensible and the intelligible.[26] In both cases ontology and phenomenology are as one, with the difference, however, that with the far from Kantian notion of categorial intuition Husserl will be drawn to put radically in question the schema upon which the *Critique of Pure Reason* was still constructed,

that of an opposition of form and matter, and to criticise, from his *On the Phenomenology of the Consciousness of Internal Time* of 1905, the distinction between apprehension and content that still formed the theoretical framework of the *Logical Investigations*. Thus he embarked, perhaps with a certain immodesty, into the depths of the *hyle* to extract the secret of the 'hidden art' recognised by Kant under the term 'transcendental schematism'. Husserl's desire not to leave ideality hovering in a void – a desire comparable with Kant's concern to give Plato's dove a support on which to take a stand (*Widerhalt*), to orient and favour its flight, i.e., the support of the sensible[27] – will lead him to consider that all idealities, whether free or 'bound' to the sensible world and to spatio-temporality, are finally 'mundane: by their historical and territorial occurrence, their "being discovered," and so on'[28] and that their a-temporality is in reality an omni-temporality, which is to say, a mode of temporality.[29]

Phenomenological idealism is thus not a philosophical taking of sides,[30] but constitutes in some way the very regime of the phenomenological mode of thought in as much as the latter renews the philosophical demand for a thought that does not renounce giving an account of its own genesis. It is perhaps already in this sense that Schelling dared to declare in 1797 that 'all philosophy is and remains idealism'.[31] It is undoubtedly what Heidegger meant in 1927 when he acknowledged that idealism has a 'primacy of principle' with respect to realism, so long as the

former is not understood as a 'psychological' idealism, and declared: 'If what the term "idealism" says, amounts to the understanding that being can never be explained by beings but is already the "transcendental" for every being, then idealism affords the only correct possibility for a philosophical problematic.'[32] Without doubt Heidegger saw at work in the transcendentalism of Husserl's 'turn' of 1907 another sense of idealism, which he judged 'no less naive in its method than the most grossly militant realism' and which involved 'tracing back every entity to a subject or consciousness whose sole distinguishing features are that it remains *indeterminate* in its being and is best characterised negatively as "un-Thing-like"'.[33] Nevertheless, he did at this period acknowledge that the "transcendental" thought of ontological difference[34] founds the 'idealist' regime of the authentic philosopher. Now, one cannot straightaway refuse Husserl access to this 'authentic' transcendentalism since through the method of the reduction – which Heidegger himself does not hesitate to borrow whilst, it is true, completing it with the addition of 'destruction' and 'construction'[35] – he had established the distinction between the given presence (the character of *Vorhandenheit*) of things experienced in the natural attitude[36] and the pure phenomenality of the world that reveals itself only in the phenomenological attitude. It becomes clear here that phenomenology does not come to be identified with a pure and simple phenomenalism and that it is only possible as 'transcendental science' involving the 'transcendence' of

the immediately given and of the distinction between this and the phenomenon-of-phenomenology. It is only on this basis that one can affirm *at once* that phenomena 'are themselves the doctrine'[37] and that, however, 'proximally and for the most part' they 'are not given'.[38]

There is therefore no phenomenology possible without reduction, implying, as Heidegger recognises, that 'just because phenomena are proximally and for the most part *not* given, there is need for phenomenology'.[39] As Husserl declared in *The Idea of Phenomenology*, the first presentation of the transcendental reduction, 'the task of phenomenology, or rather the area of its tasks and inquiries, is no such trivial things as merely looking, merely opening one's eyes'[40] since 'it is meaningless to talk about things that are simply there and only need to be seen'.[41] The task of phenomenology as Husserl understands it consists in showing how things present themselves (*darstellen*) or 'constitute' themselves in a consciousness that is no longer posited as the receptacle of their images,[42] though this *Konstituieren* (constituting) itself in no way has the sense of a making or creating but uniquely, as Heidegger emphasises, that of '*letting the entity be seen in its objectivity*'.[43] What "constitutive" phenomenology allows one to witness is the *birth* of the correlation of consciousness, and this is why it is in itself always already a 'genetic' phenomenology. There is only and could only be phenomenology where, far from installing a gulf between the 'subject' and 'object', the *res cogitans* and the *res extensa*, which only divine veracity could fill, the 'surprising' and

'essential correlation between *appearing* and *what appears*'[44] is *brought* into sight. For what is to be made visible is the unity, not to be torn apart, of the φαινομενον [phenomenon], whose double sense, at once 'subjective' and 'objective', is thus revealed and which, like the all-embracing φυσις [nature], that Heraclitus speaks of, 'likes to hide itself' in the forgetting of the self which constitutes, for the Husserlian transcendental subject as for Heideggerian Dasein, the 'natural attitude', leading it to posit the pre-sence of things and to understand itself 'inauthentically' according to the model they provide.[45]

*

Husserl is not content to situate himself only at the noetic level of transcendental phenomenology where the correlation between appearing and what appears becomes apparent, he also wants to show the very birth of this correlation, which leads him to descend to the most primitive level of hyletic phenomenology, to the 'obscure depths of the ultimate consciousness which constitutes the whole scheme of temporal existence'.[46] The 'transcendental absolute' to which the phenomenological reduction gives access, the 'noetico-noematic' correlation which allows the determination of the 'system of being closed on itself' constitutive of pure consciousness as a 'system of absolute being',[47] is in no way the last word of phenomenology that undertakes to bring into the light of day the

'ultimately and truly absolute' from whence it 'draws its radical source'.[48] And this true absolute, as Husserl indicates in a note,[49] is none other than the enigmatic 'intimacy' of consciousness and time that the 1905[50] lectures *On the Phenomenology of the Consciousness of Internal Time* describe. In effect, what Husserl is proposing is the production of 'a description of the transcendental', 'a formula in which the manifest nature of the project appears of itself' as Gérard Granel notes,[51] because it amounts to no more and no less than permitting consciousness to observe its own birth and to give birth to itself, so to speak, in what Husserl – noting the 'shocking' (*anstössig*) and even 'absurd' (*widersinnig*) character of the term – does not hesitate to term 'auto-constitution':[52] 'The flow of the consciousness that constitutes immanent time not only *exists* but is so remarkably and yet intelligibly fashioned that a self-appearance of the flow necessarily exists in it, and therefore the flow itself must necessarily be apprehensible in the flowing. The self-appearance of the flow does not require a second flow; on the contrary, it constitutes itself as a phenomenon in itself.'[53] There is here a form of *hybris* in the phenomenology of time, which claims, in contrast with the modesty of Kantian transcendentalism, to make manifest the very condition of all appearance and present it, so to speak, 'uncovered before one's eyes'.[54]

But at the same time, the phenomenology of time is, as Gérard Granel emphasises, a 'phenomenology without phenomenon',[55] since the level of *Urkonstitution*

(primal constitution) is not the level of the transparency of the Absolute to itself in the clarity of the concept but, on the contrary, that of the obscurity of the *hyle* (matter) and the original passivity of the *Urimpression* (primal impression). This original passivity can no longer be understood as that of a sensible *given*, either in a narrowly empiricist manner or even, still on the basis of the Kantian idea, of a merely sensible receptivity, but must be understood as the very mode in which the originary exists as affectivity, that is to say, as the 'passive' presentation of the thing itself in what can thus no longer be understood only as the identity of intentionality and *hyle*, of form and matter.[56] It is these 'depths', where form and matter are in one another, that Husserl terms the 'living present'. If Husserl is led to see a 'phenomenological datum' in 'the unity of the consciousness that encompasses intentionally what is present and what is past',[57] it is precisely because this act of *presentation* (*Gegenwartigen*), which comprises perception, retains within itself the past as such, which is to say absence, and because it can *present* the thing itself only by virtue of this *retention* constitutive of the act of perception as '*a single continuum that is continuously modified*' and 'is distinguished by the possession of this ideal limit', i.e., the totality of the temporal object.[58] It is this *continuity* which Husserl thinks of as 'Heraclitian flux', as the pure cometary[59] movement of a living 'now' that takes upon itself the difference between impression and retention and that precedes itself in its very own retention.[60]

One must not therefore be surprised to find that this 'metaphysics of the living present', for which, as for Bergson, there is 'change without a thing that changes'[61] and incessant modification of a flow solely constituted by a 'continuity of adumbrations',[62] lacks a language essentially:

> We can say nothing other than the following: This flow is something we speak of *in conformity with what is constituted*, but it is not 'something in objective time.' It is *absolute subjectivity* and has the absolute properties of something to be designated *metaphorically* as 'flow'; of something that originates in a point of actuality, in a primal source point, 'the now,' and so on. In the actuality-experience we have the primal source-point and a continuity of moments of reverberation. For all of this, we lack names.[63]

If we still wants to talk at this level, we must choose between a worldly logic, which indirectly names the constituent after the constituted, and a system of metaphors for the inapparent, which gives it names that are not proper ones. For what is essentially lacking at this level of *Urkonstitution* is the transcendence of the ob-ject, of the 'something in general' that becomes graspable itself only in and through naming. There is nothing to stop us understanding what Husserl here terms 'absolute subjectivity' in the manner of what Merleau-Ponty, in another context, refers

to as 'pure transcendence, without an ontic mask'[64] or even as what the late Heidegger presents as the accord of being and time in *Ereignis*[65] in the 'attempt to think being without beings' which comprises the seminar of 1962 entitled 'Time and Being'.[66] But, before taking the risk of giving a name, which would perhaps always remain metaphorical, to the un-objective, one must doubtless first know how to dwell in the nameless, as Heidegger enjoins us to do.[67] Husserl's attempt at transcendental description takes the form of the reconciliation in indifference of the extremes of absolute idealism and materialism, constitution and impression;[68] and the dialectic of impression and retention through which he endeavours to reconstruct the melodic movement of the real finally delivers – and this is the fate to which all philosophy is, through its essence, destined – only '*an ontic maquette* of ontological truth'.[69] Herein lies, in the final analysis, the signature of Husserlian phenomenology, which thus brings into the light of day what had remained hidden in the 'logical' parousia of the Hegelian absolute, that 'it steals from being what no philosophy had ever yet stolen from it, its very furtiveness, its withdrawal, its modesty, its *Gelichtetheit*',[70] by virtue of the fact that, through a perfect mimeticism, 'it succeeded in *representing* even the silence of being'.[71]

Although he saw in Platonic dialectic 'a genuine philosophical embarrassment',[72] Heidegger himself always considered the recourse to dialectic as an evasion (*Ausweg*), a manner of avoiding what is in

question, since gathering into a greater unity contradictions that have been fully accentuated in advance leaves unquestioned the opposed terms in themselves and the status of their relation. This is why Heidegger seeks to display prudence (*Vorsicht*) when engaging in the question of the relation of being and time.[73] It is this absence of precipitation and uncriticised presuppositions that leads him to posit *Ereignis* 'neither as something opposite us nor as something all-encompassing'[74] and thus to view in it neither an object nor an all-embracing absolute, since '*Ereignis* neither *is*, nor *is Ereignis there*' for 'to say the one or to say the other is equally a distortion of the matter, just as if we wanted to derive the source from the river'.[75] Perhaps it is not by chance that the image recurring here is precisely the Heraclitian, Hölderlinian and Husserlian image of the river and its source, and perhaps we ought to see in dialectics, when it is no longer an embarrassment (*Verlegenheit*) but rather an evasion (*Ausweg*), just such a perversion of the matter (*Verkehrung des Sachverhalts*) leading to the *anachronism* with which the process of becoming is reconstructed on the basis of its result. Nevertheless, such a mimetic reconstruction is in no way the last word of an impossible phenomenology but instead that against which a 'phenomenology of the inapparent' can be constituted.

What Heidegger understands under this title,[76] which has only an indicative and not a programmatic value, may initially seem just as denuded of sense and

just as shocking as the Husserlian expression 'auto-constitution' since it concerns nothing more nor less than making appear what can manifest itself, like Parmenidian being, only in an indirect manner and by virtue of a multitude of negative signs.[77] But this inapparent, which must doubtless also be understood as a 'non-signifier' after the multiplicity of meanings of the German *unscheinbar*,[78] in no way refers to some kind of absolute invisibility or, as Merleau-Ponty emphasises, to 'another "possible" *visible* or to a visible "possible" for another' but to an 'invisible which is *there*',[79] always happening *with* the visible whose secret counterpart it is. This therefore implies that with beings, being also and *at the same time* comes into presence in an inapparent manner, as moreover the participle εον (being) tells us. For, as Heidegger always insisted, αληθεια (truth) must in no way be thought of as a pre-existing *state* of openness, an immobile opening, but, on the contrary, as a robbery (*Raub*) through which a being is torn out of hiddenness,[80] or as the occurrence (*Geschehnis*) of a clearing.[81] It is this *event* – the entry into presence of what enters into presence – which a phenomenology of the inapparent such as this must examine. Now, this inappearance is equally that of the thing that never gives itself in the dimension of standing opposite and is reduced to nothing (*vernichtet*) in the absence of proximity, which is also the domination of the distanceless (*Abstandlose*), which manifests the countlessness of ob-jects as well as the measureless mass of

human beings.[82] If the thing, contrary to the indifferent object, is what touches us and concerns us (*Das Angehende*),[83] making (or letting) its inappearance appear precisely cannot result from a mere change of attitude – which is to say, from a methodological decision – but comes to pass only when 'suddenly (*jäh*), it seems, world as world worlds'.[84] The happening of the world from which the thing is lowly (*gering*) born[85] is therefore in no way the result of the methodological prudence that remains with the phenomena and abstains from giving a dialectical representation of them, even though it could doubtless not take place without its intercession. 'Method' has here only the negative virtue of preparing for what cannot be prepared for, for what, though it cannot take place *without* us, does not spring *from* us.[86] What must consequently be termed a way rather than a method takes the form of the 'step back' (*Schritt zurück*) that has the paradoxical virtue of making thought the 'fore-runner', which can lead us before the 'phenomenon' only to the extent that its merely 'provisional' essence consists uniquely 'in letting that before which it is led be seen'.[87] The backward movement is thus what makes possible the only true 'advance': the leap into the *event of presence* – which Heidegger sometimes calls *Anwesung*[88] – which does no more than lead us, through the repetition of the same accomplished by tautological thought, to where we already are, to the Parmenidian εον εμμεναι in which Heidegger sees 'the originary sense of phenomenology'.[89]

This phenomenology of the inapparent (we have yet to demonstrate that its accomplishment *necessarily* occurs in tautology inasmuch as the latter 'is the only way of thinking what dialectics can merely veil'[90]) is in the most 'pregnant' sense of the term a phenomenology of temporality, since it manifests the very interminable nature of the *movement* – or sudden leap (*Umschlag*) – from being to beings, from world to thing: of the mobility that Aristotle defined with the term μεταβολη[91] without, however, already imprisoning it in the grasping gesture of the concept.[92]

3

Logic and Metaphysics

> The real presence of the synthesis must reveal itself *immaterially*, as it were, in the language; we must become aware that, like a flash of lightning, it illuminates the latter, and like a fire flash from regions unknown, has fused the elements that needed combination.[1] (Humboldt)

The 'construction' of a phenomenological chronology, which was coupled in 1926 with the project of 'leading back' traditional logic to its philosophical sources and which resulted, in the last phase of Heidegger's thought, in the promotion of the 'sigetic'[2] form of tautological thought, itself includes the task of a 'deconstruction'[3] of the domination of logic in the philosophical mode of thought, a task that merges with the phenomenological 'destruction' of the history of ontology Heidegger assigned himself in 1927. It is already explicitly indicated in §6 of *Being and Time* that 'λεγειν is the guideline for arriving at the structure of being of the beings we encounter in speech (*Ansprechen*) and discussion (*Besprechen*)', which explains why ancient ontology first of all took the form of dialectic with Plato. It is true that following this

same passage from §6, Heidegger seems to consider Aristotle's subsequent elaboration of the hermeneutic dimension of λογος as a radicalisation[4] of dialectic which is in this way set upon the foundation of a λεγειν understood less as διαλεγεσθαι (the power to converse with his fellow man that characterises man as ζωον λογον εχον, the animal possessing λογος) than as the pure 'presentation' of something, without nevertheless the temporal structure of this λογος being explicitly recognised as such. This explains why the recognition of a hermeneutic dimension of λογος as the foundation of its dialectical 'virtue' does not remove us from the narrowness of Greek ontology that remains an ontology of ***Vor****handenheit*, of presence that has *already* come to pass, of present*ness* (*Anwesen****heit***) and not the event of coming to presence (***Anwesung***). Time itself is considered there as a being amongst others and is unknown in its ontological function, as is attested by Aristotle's treatise on time (*Physics IV*, 10-14), put forward by Heidegger in the second part of *Sein und Zeit* (*Being and Time*) as the example allowing the phenomenal basis and limits of ancient ontology to be discerned. Ancient ontology is a naive[5] ontology since it was born of the 'fallenness' of a being-in-the-world that 'proximally' and 'for the most part' is unaware of itself as such and 'naturally' tends to understand itself in terms of the world understood as a totality of pre-sent things.[6] The domination of tradition was added to the narrowness of ancient ontology, worsening the initial naivety by cutting it off from its historical roots and reducing it to

pure and simple historiographical 'material'.[7] 'Deconstruction', as Heidegger understands it, is composed of a double task: first of all 'to give back to the ossified tradition its suppleness' and 'to eliminate the successive layers with which it has been covered over time' and so to return to the 'original experiences' from which it sprang,[8] but also, and this is the *positive* aspect of *Destruktion*, to make manifest its limits with respect to the *Temporalität* (temporality) of being. It is in the context of the first of these tasks that Heidegger, in §7b of *Sein und Zeit* (*Being and Time*), the section devoted to the examination of the concept of λογος, aims to retrieve an originarily apophantic sense of this concept that precisely does not make of it the primary locus of truth.[9] What is to be explained on this basis is how the λογος αποφαντικος (apophantic λογος) will be able to become '*the* normative domain that will become the place of origin' such that 'the goal of all ontology is a doctrine of categories'.[10] Now, one cannot account for this normative status of the λογος solely on the basis of the historic [*historique*] 'sedimentation'[11] of the historial [*historial*], the process Heidegger for his part calls uprooting (*Entwurzelung*) in which the *result* of an act (the unveiling of being in the λογος) anachronically becomes unquestioned (*Selbstverständlich*) material for reworking.[12]

As historial anamnesis is the only response to historical anachronism, Heideggerian 'deconstruction' necessarily adopts the character of a retrogression (*Rückgang*) that traces back the apophantic statement,

traditionally considered to be the constitutive locus of the occurrence and preservation of truth, to the existential, hermeneutic dimension wherein its origin lies. Nevertheless, it must be emphasised that this return from the apophantic level to the properly hermeneutic level appears at this stage only as a process of tracing language back to discourse because language itself is still anachronically understood by Heidegger as the sum of words (*Wortganzheit*) and as the oral exteriorisation of discourse (*Hinausgesprochenheit der Rede*)[13] and not as one with clearing itself. It does not suffice to say that 'speech is born from meaning' to avoid considering words as things provided with meanings after the event[14] since the anteriority of a silent articulation of meanings has also been assumed, and language, which constitutes the worldly expression of discourse, then simply has the function of expressing it.[15] The distinction drawn by Heidegger between the existential level of discourse and the worldly level of language is, in fact, still tied to the same conception of language he proposes to put in question when he recalls that 'the Greek did not have a word for language' since 'they understood this phenomenon "initially' as discourse'.[16] It must be emphasised that an entire problem of meaningfulness (*Bedeutsamkeit*) had been developed within the framework of the analysis of worldhood,[17] where the *Bedeuten*, which must be understood as an 'active' signifying of Dasein with regard to itself,[18] constitutes the condition of possibility of 'meanings' of which Heidegger then

explicitly states that they 'found, in turn, the possible being of words and language'.[19] Far from adopting the point of view of a 'logico-grammatical parallelism' that sees in the categories of traditional logic the reflection of the grammatical structures of a specific language, Greek, Heidegger proposes, on the contrary, to 'free grammar from logic' and to reconstruct linguistics on a more primordial ontological foundation.[20] The λογος (semantic and phonetic articulation understood on the basis of their referential unity) has been identified, from the philosophical point of view, with the apophantic statement, and the theory of language that was subsequently constituted was constructed on this narrow 'logical' basis. Now this 'logic', as Heidegger emphasises, 'is founded on the ontology of the pre-sent being'[21] that had *separated* the hermeneutic event from the apophantic statement resulting from it and provided the latter with the *independent* existence of a fixed phonetic or grammatical semantic structure whose internal laws were then to be determined. It is on this basis that the proposition can be understood as the 'locus' of a truth that itself no longer has the sense of the 'disclosedness' of ready-to-hand beings (*Zuhandenen*) but only of the 'pre-sent conformity of a pre-sent being, of the expressed statement, *to* another pre-sent being, the being spoken about', that is to say, 'the pre-sent agreement of two pre-sent beings'.[22]

To liberate oneself from this 'logicist' interpretation of the being of language, which reached its apogee

with the theory of the 'mythical entity' of Bolzano's[23] 'proposition in itself' and was at the origin of the modern theory of truth as validity (Lotze) and value (Rickert), it is necessary – this at least is the position of Heidegger in 1927 – to undertake in the first instance an analysis of the existential structure at the origin of this unity of the double phonetic and semantic articulation, which the Greeks called λογος. Now this analysis does not take place directly in the field of discourse, an existential that does not refer to a particular temporal ecstasis,[24] but in the field of the fundamental existential of the understanding that refers to the future. For, while discourse is defined as 'the articulation of understanding',[25] articulation itself is defined as the movement of understanding in its properly projective character. This is what assures for Dasein its sight (*Sicht*) of beings, of the other Dasein and of its own being which characterises this state of openness of the there that *is* Dasein. This is why seeing an *Urphänomen* (primal phenomenon) in articulation amounts to 'taking away from pure intuition its priority which corresponds at the noetic level to the traditional ontological priority of the pre-sent being'.[26] As Heidegger emphasises, this implies that the (Kantian) distinction between intuition and thought is itself derived from the existential of understanding and is meaningful only within the limited framework of an ontology of *Vorhandenheit*.[27] It is true that the phenomenon of articulation becomes visible only in the 'development' of understanding, i.e., *Auslegung*, the interpretation which sets out [*l'explicita-*

tion qui ex-pose] a being *as* this or that, but the latter constitutes only the appropriation of what is understood and thus simply the process in which understanding becomes itself.[28] Furthermore, interpretation is one and the same as the 'simple pre-predicative seeing of the ready-to-hand'.[29] Sight thus already in itself involves understanding since interpretation does not consist in throwing the clothing of a meaning over the nakedness of a pre-sent being and sticking a value on it, but, on the contrary, has the 'specific disclosive function'[30] which implies that the articulation it institutes of the ready-to-hand being in its relation to Dasein never has 'a presuppositionless grasping of something previously given'[31] as its point of departure. This articulation of beings in relation to their being for Dasein, subsequently understood by Heidegger as the ontological difference, is what he defines as *meaning* in §32: 'When innerworldly beings are discovered with the being of Dasein, that is to say when they have come to be understood, we say that they have *meaning [Sinn]*. However, strictly speaking what is understood is not the meaning but the beings or being. Meaning is that wherein the intelligibility of something maintains itself. What can be articulated in understanding disclosure we call meaning.'[32] There is, therefore, meaning for Dasein only which does not mean that Dasein is its sovereign director since the origin of meaning, like that of language, is unassignable[33] because it is nothing other than the 'postulation' (always discovered in a retrospective manner) of an horizon on the basis of

which the grasping in return of a being *as such* becomes possible. What Heidegger here calls *Artikulation*, refers to nothing other than this 'circulation' which leads from a 'horizontal' future anterior to the 'verticality' of presence, a circularity which also constitutes the 'temporal' sense of the transcendental.[34] It is this 'circle' of understanding which is modified in the *derivative* mode of interpretation of the statement in such a way that it constitutes the formal synthetic-diaeretic structure of the predicative-determinant articulation. To determine is to *limit* understanding sight and to veil (*abblenden*) an already manifest being so as to posit it as a merely pre-sent 'subject' for it to be subsequently unveiled (*entblenden*) *in* its determinable determinateness [*le devoiler . . . en ce en quoi il est manifest*][35] through the positing of a 'predicate'. Through this modification, the *Als-struktur* (as-structure) is 'cut off from . . . its significance which constitutes the worldhood of the surrounding world' and 'forced back to the uniform level of the merely pre-sent being'.[36] Now, the λογος itself in which the predicative-apophantic articulation takes place is considered as a pre-sent being from a philosophical point of view. This is why, whilst the existential origin of articulation remains veiled, the synthetic-diaeretic structure of the statement is understood in a formal manner as the combination and/or separation of concepts in classical logic and as a pure system of relations in logistic calculus.[37] 'Logic' is thus entirely derived from the ontology of pre-sence, and it finds, in a way,

its culmination in Husserl's 'formal ontology' for which being means no more than formal being-something.[38]

*

Nearly twenty years later, in the 'Letter on Humanism', Heidegger sees in 'logic' more precisely 'the sanction, beginning with the Sophists and Plato' of 'the technical interpretation of thinking whose origins reach back to Plato and Aristotle' since 'for them thinking itself has the value of τεχνη, a process of reflection in the service of doing and making'.[39] What Heidegger now understands by 'logic' (the quotation marks are his) is no longer only the 'invention of schoolteachers and not philosophers'[40] due to Plato's and Aristotle's students and not to Aristotle himself but the properly philosophical replacement[41] of the 'sacrifice' of being as 'the element of thinking'[42] enacted by the Sophists. It is no longer a question only of 'freeing grammar from logic' but of freeing language from grammar 'to return it to a more originary essential jointure of its being' (*in ein ursprünglicheres Wesensgefüge*), a task 'reserved for thought and poetry'.[43] As Heidegger was later to declare in his course of 1951–2, 'What is Called Thinking?', 'since the course on "Logic" given in the summer of 1934' he had been led to see that 'this title "Logic" conceals "the transformation of logic into the question of the *being* of language", a question which is

something other than philosophy of language'.[44] 'Logic' and 'grammar' are now, in effect, explicitly considered as two forms of the metaphysics that took control of the interpretation of language very early in the West.[45] It emerges from these declarations that what Heidegger calls 'the metaphysical' can refer only to the occurrence of an instrumentalisation of thought and language, which is one with their 'fall' from out of the element that enables them 'properly' to be.[46] Now, in 1929, at the time when Heidegger acknowledged with Kant that metaphysics is constitutive of human nature, he already distinguished this metaphysics in the genuine sense of the term from traditional metaphysics that does not think the ontological difference.[47] This is the 'inauthentic' metaphysics which, more clearly connected with the process of the becoming scholastic of thinking become θεωρια (theory),[48] alone receives the name '*the* metaphysical'[49] in Heideggerian thinking from after the *Kehre* (turn).

If, in the last phase of his thought, Heidegger seems to locate himself 'beyond' logic and philosophy and to call for a dialogue between thinking and poetry, it is because he is devoting his efforts 'to maintaining thinking in its element'.[50] Now, this element is being and not beings, or more precisely being in its *difference* from beings, as the double sense of the participle of the Parmenidian εον already says, whereas what Heidegger calls 'the metaphysical' can, on the contrary, be considered to be 'the permanent obscuring of the question of being by the curiosity about beings', 'the ever grow-

ing sedimentation of the nominal meanings of the base participle' which have not 'ceased to obscure the primitive radiance of its verbal flash'.[51] To return thinking in this way to what is proper to it, far from establishing some kind of security for it by attaching it to an ontic certitude, consists, on the contrary, in exposing it to the 'storm of being' and the lightning flash of the event.[52] This event, viewed from and in the language of metaphysics, is above all the event of the *difference* of being and beings.[53] For metaphysics, being reveals itself 'as the ground that gives itself ground (*sich selbst ergründende*) and accounts for itself (*sich selbst begründende*)', as 'the λογος in the sense of the gathering of beings and letting them be', as the one and all, as Εν Παντα.[54] This is what Heidegger calls the *Vorprägung*, the pre-marking or pre-imprinting of being[55] from whence comes each of the historical [*historiales*] imprints outside of whose epochal event it is nothing.[56] It is this *Vor-prägung* of being by the λογος which is at the origin of the di-morphism of metaphysics, at once ontology and theology[57] since it is a thought of being at once as a generality producing the basis and traversing everything *and* as the unified totality of a rational basis and thus the highest. 'The' metaphysical is thus nothing other than the disclosing of being under the doubly unifying imprint of the λογος, the 'foundation that accounts for ground, is called to account by the ground and calls the ground to account for itself as discourse'.[58]

Thus, metaphysics paradoxically takes on the double form of an onto-logy and of a theo-logy[59] since

it is dominated by 'logic' which is a thinking of the One.[60] This logic in which metaphysics consists thinks the being *of* beings, in the double 'objective' and 'subjective' sense of the genitive (terms that themselves result from the logical imprint of being[61]), which means that it thinks the different (*das Differente*) and not difference itself,[62] the latter continuing to appear only as a distinction added by our representation to terms posited as separate and not as the 'between' on the basis of which being as well as beings appear.[63] Being and beings are not in separate places. It is being itself which transforms itself into beings through a movement of *transcendence* which is at the same time that of the arrival of beings in *presence*. This implies that they are the *same*, in the intimate intensity of the event of a split through which they are at once separated one from the other and related one to the other.[64] This is why when being and beings are thought on the basis of difference they show themselves to us on the basis of the *distributive* and *gestational* dimension that Heidegger calls *Austrag*[65] as the being apart and the being toward each other of overwhelming (*Überkommnis*) and arrival (*Ankunft*). It is this 'transversal' (*durchgängig*) dimension in relation to all the 'epochs' of being which allows us to understand that the onto-theo-logical constitution of metaphysics follows from the reign of difference from which the terms 'being' and 'beings', 'ground' and 'grounded' come. But these governing terms of metaphysics do not themselves attain the trans-epochal

dimension that appears only when, through 'the sudden lightning flash of a moment of recall in thinking', we let what has been come to language in the saying of the *Austrag*.[66] It is precisely this *letting come to language*, in opposition to the domination exercised over language by metaphysics in the form of logic and grammar,[67] which is the whole difficulty. This is because 'our western languages, each in its own way, are languages of metaphysical thinking', and the question remains open as to whether this logical 'imprint' of the being of our languages is definitive or whether they allow 'of other possibilities of speaking, that is, at the same time of a non-speaking that speaks',[68] whether, in other terms, our languages can become languages of *differance as such*, which is to say of the same,[69] having been languages of the different.

*

That the logical imprint on the being of the German language is not definitive and that it is possible to return it to a more original fittingness of its being, Heidegger's entire *oeuvre* from after the *Kehre* in itself attests since his task was constantly, not simply to 'translate' into German the governing words of philosophy,[70] but, in doing this, to prepare for a 'metamorphosis' of language that would not be the product of the fabrication of new terms, as was still the case at the time of *Sein und Zeit* (*Being and Time*),[71] but uniquely by initiating a relation to language[72]

other than that which sees in language the instrument, with a double constitution, of the ambiguous being in which the ζωον λογον εχον (animal possessing λογος) consists, i.e., Man in the metaphysical sense. The metaphysical representation of language also sees it as a being constituted by the union of a sensible element, the phonetic, and a supra-sensible element, meaning inasmuch as it exceeds the merely sensible level of the phonetic element.[73] This metaphysical representation of the essence of language doubtless still constitutes the framework of the Humboldtian definition of language as the '*work*, eternally repeating itself, *of the spirit* to render the *articulated sound* apt for the expression of *thought*'.[74] However, it is in Humboldt that one finds the idea of a metamorphosis of language that would involve neither a phonetic nor a syntactic transformation but would be uniquely *the inapparent work of time* through which 'another meaning is placed in the same abode, under the same imprint (*Gepräge*) something different is given, according to the same laws of agreement a differently arranged course of ideas is indicated'.[75]

Humboldt was the first in the Western tradition[76] to see in language not 'a simple means of exchange for the purpose of mutual comprehension', but 'a real *world* that the *spirit* must necessarily place between it and *objects* through the internal work of its force'.[77] Work, the very essence of spirit which is solely activity, is certainly, as Heidegger insists, defined here in conformity with the perspective of German

Idealism as a whole as a *Setzen*, a positing, a θεσις, which mediates and thus carries out the synthesis of subject and objects, i.e., the world. However, Humboldt's modernity and his participation in the metaphysics of subjectivity that characterises this epoch nevertheless does not prevent him from casting a penetrating glance into the heart of the deployment of the being of language,[78] as Heidegger himself recognises, since he never thinks of this mediation as posterior to the pre-existent 'realities' of subject and objects but, on the contrary, as the relation that itself constitutes the poles of subjective and objective. Humboldt insists on the fact that language, far from coming from a 'considered' act of man, possesses, on the contrary, 'a spontaneity (*Selbstthätigkeit*) which is visibly manifest to us even though it is inexplicable in its being'. Since it springs 'from a depth of humanity that forbids us for ever from considering it as a genuine work and creation of peoples' one must see it as 'not a product of activity but an involuntary emanation of the spirit, not a work of nations but the gift that their internal destiny has given them' because 'they use it without knowing how they have formed it'.[79]

This world which is 'posited' between the subject and the object can therefore appear only in the contingent singularity of its 'intersubjective' creation in the wake of a reflexive look since this creation is the work of a spirit still unconscious of itself whose auto-activity must, paradoxically, be understood as the passivity of

an 'involuntary' outpouring.[80] With this, the fundamental *temporality* of what German idealism thinks of under the terms 'positing' and 'synthesis' can be glimpsed. Now, this 'synthesis', to the extent that it comes to pass as language – that is to say, as speech [*parole*], *Sprache*, since what in French, as in Greek, Latin and English is named on the basis of the organ of speech, the tongue [*langue*], γλωσσα, *lingua*, language, German names on the basis of the verb *sprechen*, to speak[81] – is the 'synthesis' of sound and thought whose 'mutual accord' Humboldt celebrates in passages of great beauty.[82] His conception of *Sprache* is characterised by the emphasis placed upon the originarily corporeal character of articulation understood as resting upon 'the power exercised by the spirit on the organs of speech controlling their handling of the phonetic element that corresponds to the form of its action'.[83] *Sprache* is considered by Humboldt, from the perspective of Romanticism's speculative principle of Organicism,[84] as 'the organ that gives form to thought', which is to say, as that which, through the intermediary of the phonetic element (*Laut*), gives material exteriority and phenomenal sensibility to 'intellectual activity that passes in a manner completely spiritual, completely interior and, so to say, without leaving a trace'.[85] The articulation of the voice (*Stimme*) in linguistic sound (*Sprachlaut*) thus embodies time, renders the interior exterior and the spiritual material. If it is true that Humboldt understands language at once on the basis of the mouth and the ear, seeing in it

the movement of 'the spiritual aspiration forcing its way past the lips' and 'returning to its own ear in the form of what it had produced',[86] and if he celebrates 'the happy organisation of hearing and the organs of speech',[87] it remains the case that articulation, as constitutive of 'the proper being of language', must be understood in its birth and not in its result,[88] which is to say as a pure originary formative activity that is as one with intention and the capacity of meaning,[89] disconnected from its auditive reception.[90] Semantic articulation and phonetic articulation can therefore be distinguished only in an abstract manner since 'the indissoluble alliance that ties thinking, the vocal organs and hearing to language rests unchangingly on the originary organisation (*Einrichtung*) of human nature which is not itself susceptible to explanation'.[91]

It is therefore the 'living resonance' of the voice, springing from the human lungs, which 'through incessantly repeated actions, ties together in itself the world and man, or, in other terms, his spontaneity and receptivity'.[92] It becomes clear here that Humboldt perceives the actuality of the 'hidden art' of the Kantian schematism in the articulation of the φωνη σεμαντικη (meaningful sound) itself. However, this synthesis of the internal linguistic form and the phonetic element which so decisively allies language with an art[93] is neither an existing quality nor a determined action, it is much rather 'an always transitory and instantaneous effective action' which does not reveal itself by any particular sign, not even words. This is why Humboldt

compares it in its immateriality to a flash of lightning which illuminates language and which, 'like a fire come from unknown regions has fused together the materials to be combined'[94]. This 'act of synthetic positing' (*Act des synthetischen Setzens*), differing from Kantian cognitive synthesis which remains dependent upon an *exterior* objectivity through the bias of the receptivity of sensibility, is an 'act of spontaneous positing through concentration' (*Act des selbstthätigen Setzens durch Zusammenfassung*) which, constantly repeating itself in language, produces for itself its own objectivity in the materiality of articulated sound: 'Spirit creates, but *in the very act* stands over against (*stellt gegenüber*) what it has created and lets it, as an object, work on it in return (*zurückwirken*). In this way is born, on the basis of the world reflected in man, between one and the other, what attaches one to the other and enriches one by the other: language.'[95] It is this action upon itself of a creative spontaneity which allows Humboldt to define, in a more authentically Aristotelian sense than Heidegger thinks,[96] language as ενεργεια, as activity bearing its own 'product' within itself but capable *at the same time* of standing over against it, as if it were its other, through an infinite reiteration and a rhythmic caesura that marks the very words of inflected languages.[97] For, 'there are in effect points, in the grammatical structure of languages, in which this synthesis and the force that produces it are, so to speak, illuminated in a more naked and more immediate way'[98] and, amongst the three 'points' that

allow the recognition of the vigour of the synthetic act, the verb, the conjunction and the relative pronoun, 'the verb alone is the central point that encompasses and spreads life', whilst 'all the other terms of the sentence are, so to speak, dead material, waiting for a connection' since with the verb the synthesis of the predicate with the subject passes from simple thought to the actuality of a real process: 'We do not think the flash of lightning only, it is the lightning itself which strikes here; we are no longer content to bring together spirit and the imperishable to unite them, rather spirit is the imperishable. Thinking, if we may express ourselves in such figurative fashion, leaves its interior resting place and makes its entry into the actuality of the real.'[99]

4

The Logos of Mortals

> The essential relation between death and language, a lightning flash, lights up; but it is still unthought.[1] (Heidegger)

Western Metaphysics, at its height, is a thinking of work and of the eternal repetition of spirit, and it understands itself, with Humboldt, as the experience of the undying flow of time in the inflected modulations of saying. This thought of the *Unvergänglichen*, the immortal, does not, however, lack the anti-rhythmic moment of caesura in which the confrontation of death at the very interior of life consists since it is the very menace of mummifying objectification[2] which revives the always recommenced work of spirit. As Hegel emphasises, it is 'the tremendous power of the negative', 'the energy of thinking, of *pure I*', which allows 'the accidental' to be given 'an existence of its own and a separate freedom', as 'what is tied and is actual only in its context with others', since 'the life of spirit' is not 'the life that shrinks from death and keeps itself untouched by devastation' but, on the contrary, it is the life that 'endures it and maintains itself in it'.[3] In effect, spirit is 'powerful' only if it has the 'magical power' of 'converting the negative into being',[4] implying

that it is not 'a passive subject inertly supporting accidents', but 'the self-moving concept which takes its determinations back into itself'.[5] Now, in this movement of conversion and of renewal, the immobile subject 'collapses', and it is *this inflection itself that becomes the object.*[6] In this way, what has the form of the predicate in a sentence is no longer the universal applicable to more than one thing because it does not exist 'by itself' and, as an attribute, is always in something else. Rather, it is substance itself and so presents itself as separate.[7] Representational thought (*das vorstellende Denken*), which is nothing other than 'logical' thought in its traditional definition, thus becomes 'hindered in its progression' across predicates by the 'counter-thrust' it undergoes and that transforms it from a judgement containing the difference between subject and predicate into an identical proposition. But the philosophical proposition cannot stay with this result, with identity alone: it must contain the passage itself, which is to say the 'counter-thrust' of the second proposition against the first, implying that 'the identity of subject and predicate is not meant to destroy the difference between them, which the form of the proposition expresses; their unity, rather, is meant to emerge as a harmony'.[8]

We are here, in effect, at the level of 'dialectical movement', in the 'element of the pure concept',[9] and the latter finds its being-there [*être-là*] only in time,[10] implying that the movement of thinking cannot rest on any pre-existing content. There is therefore no

'underlying subject' which a predicate might befall, since the content is here 'in its own self, subject through and through'.[11] One must not remain in interior inhibition expressed by thought satisfying itself with a dead identity and coming to a stop. Rather, to prevent the form of the proposition being sublated [*abolie*] (*aufgehoben*) in a merely immediate fashion 'this opposite movement must be expressed (*ausgesprochen*)' and 'the return of the concept into itself must be *presented* (*dargestellt*)' in syllogistic proof, without which we simply fall back upon simple '*inner* intuition' without attaining 'the speculative in act'.[12] The springing up of the harmonious unity of subject and predicate therefore demands expression, linguistic *Aussprache*, and exposition, logical *Darstellung*. It demands that the return of essence into itself take the form of being-there,[13] implying that difference and exteriority are not immediately absorbed again into identity. This is what Hegel himself calls 'the immanent rhythm of the concept'[14] in which thinking must not arbitrarily intervene but whose tension it must take upon itself through a wise abstention.[15] There is no rhythm without conflict, and here it is a question of the rhythm of the dual form of the proposition destroyed by the unity of the concept. Hegel compares it to that of metre and accent in poetic rhythm, which results as much from the suspense of the interval that separates them as from their reunion.[16] This rhythm which expresses the life of the concept is termed *Widerspruch*, contradiction, and, as Heidegger recalls,

Hegel says of it in the *Logic* that 'it is the root of all movement and of all life; it is only to the extent that something contains a contradiction within itself that it moves, that it possesses a force of impulsion and an activity'.[17] Now, this activity is constantly thought of as the power of objectivisation, as the capacity of self-representation through reflection, which explains why the dialectic or the speculative[18] are defined by Hegel as 'the grasping of op-posites in their unity or of the positive in the negative'.[19] It is the production of op-posites that Hegel understands precisely as 'work'. The dialectical process can therefore become 'the fundamental movement in the totality of the objectivity of all objects, which is to say of being such as it is understood by the moderns',[20] only to the extent that speculative identity can only ever be realised from the point of view of a 'productive' subject. It is true that the young Hegel already sought in Schelling's philosophy of identity a construction of the absolute in the subject which would no longer produce itself solely from a subjective point of view, as with Fichte, but also from an objective point of view. But this inquiry in itself implies that Hegel continued to conceive of the absolute as such a subject capable of 'finding *itself* in absolute diremption' because, as he explicitly says, the 'magic force' that converts the negative into being 'is the same thing as what had above been termed subject'.[21]

Is there deep within dialectic, which Heidegger himself judges to be 'in certain respects the highest'

'dimension' of thinking,[22] the possibility of letting the thing *itself* come to language without recourse to the permanence of a subject proving necessary? Or, can the thought of dia-chrony deploy itself only, as the Hegelian example demonstrates, in the form of a *Science of Logic*, that is to say as an 'onto-logy of absolute subjectivity'[23] whose *logos* remains, right up to its speculative presentation, marked by the predicative structure and the opposition of object and subject? To pursue this question, one would have to interrogate the figure who, well before Hegel and Schelling, undertook to locate the Fichtian principle of the I in relation to a higher unity, that of '*Sein schlechthin*', of 'simple being'.[24] In a short essay entitled 'Judgement and Being', written at the beginning of 1795 when he was an auditor of Fichte's in Jena, Hölderlin emphasises that the order of being that 'expresses the connection between subject and object' constitutes the necessary presupposition of all reflection. Against Fichte, who understands the identity of the I as coming from a self-positing of the I, he shows that 'the I [*moi*] is only possible thanks to the separation of the I [*je*] from the I [*moi*]', implying that the I is in no way an absolute identity but the identity of the opposed I-subject and I-object only. For, identity is a concept of reflection only, and it is consequently impossible to see the truth of Spinozan substance in the I, as Fichte wanted to. One must therefore not confuse being with identity, the sphere of the reflexive scission with that of the unification of subject and object in being. All of

Hölderlin's subsequent reflections were to consist in thinking the union, in a genetic sense, of these two spheres which constitute the poles of a dynamic unity, of a 'life' at once human and divine that is only ever realised in a finite concrete figure since there is neither a general essence of life, nor a general essence of thinking, nor a universal spirit.[25] In this way, Hölderlin encounters, with the whole of German idealism, the genetic unity of opposites already expressed in Heraclitus's fragment 119 which speaks of the opening of human dwelling to the manifestation of the divine and which, rediscovered by German mysticism, led Nicholas of Cusa to the idea of a *coincidentia oppositorum*. However, what constitutes the peculiarity of Hölderlin's thought is that this genesis is seen in its *simultaneity* with decline, which is to say no longer against the kinetic horizon of the persistence of a subject capable of 'bearing' [*supporter*] the accident of its own death which makes all genesis a γενεσις τις, a genesis of something, but against the metabolic horizon of the γενεσις απλως, of genesis understood as being in its most simple sense as the pure 'unmotivated' passage from non-being to being. What Hölderlin wants to think is not the development of a thing from its initial stage to its final stage, even via the intermediary of a 'qualitative leap' which would introduce here a relative discontinuity, but rather the entire reflux of disappearance into appearance and of death into life. What he wants to understand is not the succession of epochs and the interval that separates the breaks but the

epochal break itself and the radical discontinuity of history.

In an essay that has legitimately been given the title 'Becoming in Dissolution',[26] Hölderlin deploys a thought of history that sees in it the unique 'site' of the always singular birth of the absolute and not that of its 'Calvary' only, as is the case for Hegel whose dialectic, to the extent it raises Christianity to the level of a 'philosopheme', has the 'sacrificial' structure of the infinite that, because it exists before the finite, must manage to find itself again through death and resurrection in the latter.[27] For Hölderlin, perishing comes *first* from an ontological point of view and 'becoming in perishing' is the ontological form of the 'being' of the infinite, to the extent that the latter is 'produced' (*sich herstellt*) only in decline and passage.[28] The infinite can be found only in the 'passage' itself from a world or an epoch to another whose unforeseen 'springing up' authorises no globalising logicisation. Each epoch is thus in itself the most accomplished presentation of the infinite, and the latter can be seized only in a flash of lightning in the 'genetic moment' of the coincidence of the death and the birth of a world, in the joyous mourning and the feeling of total life that is the experience in perishing of the structural unity of the infinite and the finite, of actual life and of the superior life and thus of the process of representation [*figuration*] perpetually creative of life. This memorial interiorisation of the real dissolution called 'ideal dissolution' by Hölderlin enacts a return

from the present to the past, from the infinite to the finite. It has a properly restitutive dimension which is why what is lived as weakening or death is *in itself* (and not only in its result) the reviving and growth of what has been, not destructive violence but love that enhances, understands, conserves what has been.[29] This process of elevation, in which the present gains in spirit to the extent that it gives spirit to the past, is the creative act in which the 'subject', neither divine nor human, of the historical process consists. Hölderlin insists on this point at the end of the essay, it is only in the tragic union of finite and infinite that perpetually creative life is conserved. Epochs constitute themselves in opposition to one another such that they are unified in a tragic manner only, that is to say they can in no way be unified from a 'reconciliatory' teleological point of view but only conserved and placed in relation with each other in what Hölderlin calls *Vereinigung*, the union that retains the opposed elements, turning them towards one another and maintaining them in a reciprocal tension. Such a thought, whose ground is *Grunderfahrung*, the fundamental experience of the *presence* of the infinite in the finite, is opposed to metaphysical logic which, on the contrary, conceives of the finite as contained in the infinite. But this *presence*, because it is properly experienced only in the lightning flash of its disappearance, opens the clearing of its possible re-production only in always new finite forms. It is against this horizon that language can appear as the very paradigm of the

'genetic' phenomenon,[30] in the sense that in it particularity and totality, infinite and finite, sound and sense are intimately united.

*

Since it is a thought of singularity and discontinuity, Hölderlin's restitutive dialectic thus remains faithful to the earliest sense of διαλεγεσθαι, that of plural speech and the actuality of engaging in dialogue with one another. Hölderlin speaks in '*Friedensfeier*' ('Celebration of Peace') of this dialogue (*Gespräch*) we are, specifying, however, that 'soon we shall be song'.[31] That the *Gespräch* must become *Gesang*[32] and that dialectical logic manages to experience itself as the 'poetic logic' that Hölderlin speaks of at the beginning of the *Remarks on Antigone* is perhaps constitutive of the most intimate 'destination' of language which, by combining in this way its thinking component with its acting component, its semantics and its syntax, would reunite what, since the beginning of philosophy, has been separated into επιστημη (knowledge) and ποιησις (making). Since, as Hölderlin emphasises, while philosophy, under the name logic, only ever treats *one* faculty of the *soul*, poetry treats the *various* faculties of man.[33] Now, the latter must be understood in the Kantian manner as constituting in its entirety a 'system of receptivity' wherein representation, sensation and reasoning occur successively.[34] And, it is 'the coherence of the most autonomous elements of the diverse faculties'

of the human being, in contrast with 'the simple coherence of the articulations' of the unique faculty of the soul, i.e., the understanding, which 'can be called rhythm in the higher sense'.[35] It is clear from this definition of rhythm that the latter constitutes the cohesion (*Zusammenhang*) of a successive diversity, each element of which manifests a tendency towards autonomy, towards *Selbständigkeit*. The compound rhythm of the Hegelian logic of the concept is deployed as the movement of beings themselves in their becoming other with regard to themselves and as the return on the basis of their being-there to the simplicity of auto-determination, a circularity which testifies that the content of Science 'has not received its determination from something else'.[36] Being itself has thus reabsorbed into itself its own strangeness since it makes of itself λογος. To this simplicity (*Einfachheit*) of the conceptual rhythm of the Odyssey of spirit, Hölderlin opposes the halting and 'unbound' (*ungebundenste*)[37] character of tragic rhythm which – like Dionysus, the 'fruit of the storm' born of the divine lightning flash that reduced Semele[38] to ashes – is engendered in the 'coupling' of God and man that comes to pass in the 'dialogue constantly in conflict', i.e., human speech.[39] The tragic is born of the 'monstrous' experience of the encounter with the wholly other, with what can be 'harmonised' only in a non-manifest[40] manner like the yawning gap that opens between earth and sky before one who, standing upright, casts a look outside.[41]

It is this 'secret of the encounter'[42] that, in an in-

apparent manner, manifests the 'music' of human speech in the διαλεγειν that originally defines it. For, 'speaking with one another, in its fine flower, διαλεγειν in the double sense [of speaking with one another and listening to one another] is the mother tongue as dialect. . . . The being of language [*das Sprachwesen*] is rooted in dialect. While the manner of the mouth (*die Mundart*) is the mother tongue, what constitutes the familiarity (*das Heimische*) of one's home (*die Heimat*) is also rooted in it. Dialect is not simply the mother tongue, but it is at the same time and above all the mother of language.'[43] Heidegger recognises here that dialectic draws its primary sense from the originally dialectical character of language which defines the intrinsic historicity and locality of the latter, to the point that the very notion of 'place of birth', of *Heimat*, draws its sense only from this character of language: the long text of 1960, '*Sprache und Heimat*' ("Language and Home"), devoted once again to the Alemanic poet Johann Peter Hebel, ends on the transformation of the title into 'Sprache *als* Heimat', 'Language *as* home', since 'poetic saying alone lets mortals dwell *on* the earth, *under* the heavens and *before* the gods'.[44] On the basis of such a dialectical being of language it is possible to understand what the *voice* is by no longer relating it either to the horizon of a physiological explanation of phoneticism or to the metaphysical horizon of the self-presence of a subject. What Humboldt, in a not undivided manner, still calls *Sprachlaut*, the sound of speech, must be understood

on the basis of the very intonation of the voice, of the resonance of its *Stimmen*, which retains within itself *against* the void of the heavens the obscurity and the withdrawal of the earth.[45] It is this agreement which grants that which rises up together with its time, the lightning flash of the *Gleich-zeitigkeit*, the simultaneity, of the ecstasies of time, on the basis of which alone the space of the world opens up.[46]

Epilogue

Lightning governs all things. [1] (Heraclitus)

Chrono-logy interrupts itself at the very moment it makes manifest the lightning flash of the simultaneity that makes it possible since with it, as philosophers[2] just as much as poets have said, what we call the beginning is often the end, the end is where we start from.[3] In this way, the *truth* of transcendentalism, at once evasive and founding, of the archeo-teleology of philosophy, resides from the chrono-logical point of view in the opening of the space of a possible encounter that itself always takes place in the instantaneousness of a 'present' where we are to dwell in improvisation since it is, as Heidegger emphasises, what we are waiting for in coming to our encounter and what we ordinarily call the future.[4] This regressive path, this Odyssey of philosophy, whose entire virtue consists in leading us back to where we always already, though improperly, are, has, however, only the circular form of absolute reflection because it ecstatically opens us to the outside of the world, according to the reversibility dear to Merleau-Ponty, for whom 'leaving oneself is returning to oneself and visa versa'.[5] And it is this circle, which we rightly call

'hermeneutic', that paradoxically makes us capable of welcoming the surprise of the event whose unforeseeable nature takes off from the ground of our anticipations, as if through excess.

It is doubtless this surprise that is the origin of speech and the very essence of the voice. Since speech is torn from us in an abduction, it springs up only from us, in spite of ourselves, and ties us to ourselves by taking the immense detour of the world, and the voice is in itself only the phenomenon of the auto-hetero-affection by virtue of which, as Aristotle[6] already affirmed, the human soul opens itself to the strangeness of beings and the for-itself welcomes alterity. The voice will therefore always be the name of this element in the human that decentres the human[7] and opens it to what it is not. The synchrony through which alone ipseity can be constituted does not come to pass for its own benefit but, on the contrary, to transport us ecstatically to the point where this happens to us and, in happening, literally places us in the world. This is why time is presented to us, in the interrupting experience of the encounter, at one go and like a flash of lightning and why it appears in this way not only, as the poets clearly perceived, in its entirety[8] but also in the paradoxical immobility that the philosophers have in turn been able to recognise in it.[9] However, at this point of indifference where there comes to pass the lightning flash of the belonging together of the human and of being, called *Ereignis*[10] by Heidegger, the impossible alliance of receptivity and spontaneity, of activity and passivity, takes place

or more precisely it *gives* rise to the plurality of rhythms and times, to the multiplicity of beings and things. But that, doubtless, only a poet could express:

> At the still point of the turning world. Neither flesh nor fleshless;
> Neither from nor towards; at the still point, there the dance is,
> But neither arrest nor movement. And do not call it fixity,
> Where past and future are gathered. Neither movement from nor towards,
> Neither assent nor decline. Except for the point, the still point,
> There would be no dance, and there is only the dance. [11]

In our Western languages, so strongly marked by the stamp of metaphysics and in which the constraints exercised by the grammatical functions give such a great importance to predication and the notion of the subject,[12] is it possible to let the silent event of the encounter come to language? What cannot be said can perhaps be read backwards on the back of a writing that tirelessly celebrates the mourning of presence in the infinite dissemination of signs.[13] But it is perhaps also possible directly to *make* a sign – in the sense of *Wink* and not of *Zeichen*[14] – towards the event in the silences of a restrained speech and through the grace come to pass of a metamorphosis, not of language, but

of our relation to language where 'the rigour of thinking, carefulness in saying and frugality with words find a wholly other credit than that they have so far received'.[15]

At this time when everyone is instructed to publish the most minor drafts, when there are already more supposed authors than genuine readers, and when thinking, forgetting that its nocturnal source lies in the assumption of mortality, associates itself ever more with journalism and succumbs to the illusion of the transcendence of history, it is more important than ever to recall that the thinker, just like the poet, 'is notable according to the quantity of insignificant pages that he does not write'[16] and that all speech, in the extreme risk of its utterance, comes about only as a homage to the silence the hearing of which, if possible, is its sole vocation.

A Note on the Bibliography

Tradition dictates that a thesis be accompanied by a bibliography. Nevertheless, I have not judged it necessary to conform to this practice, given the abundance – doubtless excessive – of notes added to the preceding text. Yet, it has always seemed extremely important, and this applies, in my view, to all attempts at thinking, not to fail to cite one's sources. This duty is all the more pressing the less 'powerful' the thought is and the less it claims to 'found' the edifice of an 'original' mode of thinking. This is why the absence in this place of a detailed bibliography signifies less negligence or insolence than it attests, on the contrary, that this brief adverbial text has no other pretension than to 'dwell' in the interstices of a tradition which, for me, it is not a question of 'refuting' or even of 'renewing' but simply of *making appear* in the light of a question, that of time, in the hope of seeing it open *in itself* and *by itself* to other traditions of *thinking*, on this basis. In any case, I have always located the Heideggerian critique of metaphysics in this perspective, inasmuch as it remains inseparable from the taking up of a 'heritage' truly ours only because, in its living traditional nature, it 'is preceded by no testament'.[1] For, to end on another line of René Char's rightly associated on more than one

occasion by Jean Beaufret with Heideggerian *Destruktion*:

Finally, if you destroy, let it be with nuptial tools.[2]

Appendix

Chrono-logies[1]

Can one tell the lightning flash of presence? Such is the question that had already formed in me at my *lycée*, while, following the advice of my teacher, Monique Dixsaut, I plunged at the same time into reading Bergson's *Thought and Movement* and Nietzsche's *The Will to Power* in Geneviève Bianquis's translation. It seemed to me then that poetry alone could manage, through the extreme condensation of saying which it accomplishes, to express the movement of the real, the 'change without a thing that changes' Bergson speaks of, since, as Nietzsche showed clearly, the 'metaphysical grammar' of philosophy consists in doubling the event of becoming with a second world peopled with substrates and imaginary entities.

An encounter with phenomenology, to which I was initiated, variously, by Paul Ricoeur and Jacques Derrida, then teaching at the Sorbonne, revived this question several years later. It was therefore less in the context of a radical critique of ontology, following the Nietzschian model which sees in being only a 'vapour of a word', than in the Husserlian and above all Heideggerian horizon of a *phenomenological ontology*

that I was drawn to formulate the same inquiry in the Master's dissertation I devoted in 1966 to 'Language and Ontology in Heidegger', under the direction of Paul Ricoeur. I saw in this phenomenological ontology no longer the *science* of being identified with what Heidegger, following Husserl, calls *Vorhandenheit*, the subsistence or already accomplished pre-sence of a substrate-being, that, as such, can inhabit only the beyond of a second world, but the *coming to language* of being in the verbal sense which is identical to the very occurrence of time and refers to no other rule than to that of phenomenality.

In this way I was led, taking as my guiding thread the Heideggerian attempt to 'reform' the language of metaphysics, to a lasting interest in the status of the discursivity proper to the Western mode of thought as it rests on the predicative proposition and is tied to a determinate conception of philosophical logic. The question of the possibility of a use of language and of a phenomenological logic that would be given over to the 'temporality of being' had then become the principal axis of my reflection. After entering the university as an assistant, it seemed necessary to give this question the academic form of a subject of a *thèse d'état* that I entitled, in a fairly vague manner, 'Heidegger and Language' and that Paul Ricoeur, in spite of the imprecise nature of the project, agreed to supervise exactly twenty years ago, at a time when his 'Phenomenology and Hermeneutics' seminar in the Avenue Parmentier in Paris was the place where I

really worked. I must admit that I had at the time fallen victim to the illusion that consists in believing oneself to be the owner of a theme and the inventor of a question, and it was in this condition that I busied myself, in the following years, amassing material for what was to have taken the form of a longwinded academic work.

I had still not at this point realised the extent of the irony that governs every enterprise of thinking and of the immense naivety that pushes us to imagine ourselves the masters of our own questions, when it is they that in reality lead us at times even where we do not wish to go. Many years and the conjunction of various circumstances were required before I saw that I could not accomplish the project of a thesis on Heidegger. The analysis, pursued throughout this period, of what is often described, in the context of what Nietzsche would with some right call 'an antique dealer's historicism', as the 'corpus' of an author had led me in a more and more decisive manner to consider Heidegger's work less as constituting an object of study in itself than as an invitation to what he calls a *Gespräch*, a dialogue with the thinkers. By scrupulously following Heidegger's indications I found myself engaged in reading not only the fundamental texts, Greek and German, of Western thought but also the thinkers belonging in a broad sense to the 'phenomenological' movement. From then on, it was out of the question to envisage giving a finished form to an inquiry that promised indeed to be interminable.

Anyway, the inquiry was its own justification since it was more than enough to secure the enjoyment intrinsic to that celebration in which the mere exercise of thinking consists, an activity which has no need of exteriorisation in works.

It was in this frame of mind – a frame of mind that I like to think of as eminently philosophical, philosophy being nothing other for me than the practice of teaching with respect to which Heidegger rightly emphasised that it is the teacher who learns the most – that I decided to renounce the project of the monumental French *thèse d'état*, all the while being acutely conscious of having in this way failed to fulfil the tacit contract that tied me to the institution. However, this decision did allow me henceforth to accept invitations to give lectures and write articles in which I risked presenting a brief synthesis of the readings I had undertaken and brought out the nodal points of what it is the fashion to call philosophical 'research', although it seemed to me personally to be more like meditation and even, more prosaically, that 'rumination' spoken of by Nietzsche. Especially as regards the last ten years of my 'work' (another fashionable term), it is clear that, far from forming a disparate miscellany, its parts are so closely interrelated that, although treating different topics and authors, they are exposed to the danger of repetition. It would therefore be wrong to see this sequence of texts as stages of a philosophical itinerary leading to a destination. They should be regarded rather as a kind of running on the

spot in a frequently repeated attempt to seize in the overlapping of their various aspects the complex configuration of a question which remains perennially the same.

These then are the 'exercises' or 'essays' which I am now going to endeavour to 'defend', since Jacques Taminiaux's generous invitation to be your guest here and to give a résumé of my work persuaded me that the time had come for me to settle, in my own way, the debt I bore to the institution called the University. Nowhere seems to me more appropriate for this than Louvain whose name is so closely associated with phenomenology and where the latter has always remained a living form of thought, in particular in the Centre for Phenomenological Studies, presided over by Jacques Taminiaux, whose work I have followed from afar. It must be said again, following Heidegger, that phenomenology constitutes not merely a 'point of view' or a 'trend' in philosophy but the only method appropriate to it, a view perfectly expressed by the Husserlian maxim of the return to things themselves. 'Phenomenology' is for me – this would be my first 'thesis', the one underpinning all the others – the 'true' name of a philosophy concerned less with searching for the truth 'behind' appearances than with opening itself to the donation *hic et nunc* of being that, far from isolating us under the figure of an absolute without ties, is, on the contrary, in its finitude nothing other than the relation it has to us. This 'phenomenology of finitude', in Jan Patočka's elegant formula, can, in

contrast with Hegelian phenomenology, be built only by breaking with the idea of an absolute mastery of phenomenality. I saw this at work, *par excellence*, in Heidegger's thinking, without this ever distancing me from the assiduous reading of Husserl's texts to which I was introduced in a decisive manner just as much by the abundant notes accompanying Paul Ricoeur's translation from 1950 of the *Ideas*, as by the long commentary on *The Origin of Geometry* published by Jacques Derrida in 1962.

Talk of a phenomenological 'movement' and not a 'school' is well founded, and I have always tried to stay in this movement, joining rather than opposing the names Husserl and Heidegger, by following the example of those who have found themselves 'caught' between the two thinkers and who have worked, admittedly not without difficulty, to maintain the unity of phenomenology: Eugen Fink, Jan Patočka and, in France, Merleau-Ponty. One can, as the last of these clearly showed, unilaterally see in Husserlian phenomenology a philosophy of intentionality which would display the absolute mastery of meaning by the subject but one must also recognise the marks, in particular under the terms 'operative intentionality' and 'passive genesis', of a discourse of the non-presence of the subject to itself, decisively opening the latter to temporal transcendence. This is why reading Husserl's texts constitutes for me not only the 'school of rigour' it is rightly agreed to be and through which it is a good thing to pass but also a permanent

dwelling place. It seemed to me essential, in the short essays I have devoted to Husserl, not only to emphasise the considerable enlargement the notion of intuition undergoes in the sixth *Logical Investigation*, a crucial point for Heidegger who saw in categorial intuition the point of departure for his own question of being, but also, in a less strictly Heideggerian manner, to place emphasis upon everything that prevents one from considering transcendental phenomenology to be a simple repetition of Cartesianism: on the importance and precocity in Husserl's thought of the problem of intersubjectivity, on the wholly singular nature of his idealism which links him to a 'true' positivism and above all to his critique of the thing in itself and the Kantian theory of the two modes of intuition, originary and derivative, which lead him, by refusing to accept the idea of an actual infinite, to confer on time, in a strange proximity to Nietzsche, a wholly new ontological importance since the supposed eternity of idealities and logical truths is revealed to be only an omni-temporality, which is to say a mode of temporality.

Refusing to play off Heidegger against Husserl in this way, my reflections developed in two complementary directions at once: the investigation of the Husserlian foundation of a 'pure logic' and the theory of meaning underpinning it inasmuch as it is the corollary of a genetic problem in phenomenology that leads at the level of the *Krisis* to the idea of a paradoxical historicity of truth; and the analysis of the

Heideggerian *Destruktion* of the theory of language and traditional logic that should be understood less as the rejection of logic and the promotion of irrationality than as a leading back of traditional logic to its temporal foundations, which is to say to a larger sense of λογος than that which confines it within the structure of the predicative proposition.

To do this required first of all the clarification of the very framework of Heidegger's thought, and this is what I attempted to set out in a short book published in 1990 on *Heidegger et la question du temps*.[2] Since 1927 Heidegger's project had in no way been that of inscribing his fundamental question in the already circumscribed field of philosophy but, on the contrary, of questioning the condition of possibility of the latter and of exposing the roots of Western rationality. Philosophy was determined with Plato and Aristotle as the form of thought that claims to account for what is *presently* given, for beings as such, without appealing to an origin of another order and, in this way, breaking with the mythological mode of thought. From that moment Heidegger's question concerned the condition of possibility of the understanding of being as *constant presence* in the Greek philosophers and their heirs. What makes possible the understanding of being on the basis of a specific dimension of time, the present? Such, in its most raw sense, is the question at the origin of *Being and Time*. Heidegger did not seek to oppose time and becoming to being, nor did he see in the latter the 'meaningless fiction'

that Nietzsche saw. On the contrary, he sought to bring out the secret connection of what we call 'being' with time. What makes the rational discourse of Western logic possible is a certain understanding of being against the horizon of time governing the comportment of that being, open to itself and to other beings, which Heidegger calls Dasein and whose intrinsic temporality defines it as being essentially towards death. It is therefore the finite temporality of existence which is the source of the idea of being on which Western rationality is founded. What is thus brought out is that philosophy is never a 'pure' theory and that ontology can never be detached from its concrete existential root. The science of being is consequently a *temporal* science that can in no way be founded on the a-temporality of reason nor on the eternity of truth, two fundamental presuppositions of traditional logic.

From this latter perspective of an inquiry into the meaning of the supremacy of logic in Western thought, I then directed my work, above all in the framework of my teaching, towards German Idealism and, in particular, Hegelian dialectical logic since the latter presents itself as the most powerful attempt to submit being to the imperatives of reason. The identification in Hegel of logic and ontology nevertheless takes the form of an overcoming of traditional logic and of its founding principles: the principles of identity and non-contradiction. But this recognition of contradiction as the motor of the dialectical mode of

thought takes place in the context of the predicative proposition which, far from being brought into question, continues to form the fundamental structure of the speculative proposition in which subject and predicate merely swap positions. The Hegelian dialectic thus manifests the culmination of the thesis of the logical nature of being in which Nietzsche was to see the very essence of metaphysics.

Is there not, however, another mode of thought that, while giving a place to contradiction or rather to conflict, nevertheless does not present itself as the leading back of the λογος αποφαντικος [apophantic λογος], on which the entire edifice of traditional logic rests but constitutes rather a radical questioning of it? It was by posing this question that I was drawn to interest myself in Hölderlin's theoretical essays more than in his poetry, following in this also an indication of Heidegger's who saw in Hölderlin one who had penetrated and broken the speculative Idealism Hegel had worked to constitute. The short work which I devoted to Hölderlin's reflections on tragedy[3] and which, like almost the entirety of the writings presented here, is the text of lectures, is really only a fragment of a much larger project that attempted to bring out the specificity of Hölderlin's mode of thought inasmuch as it comes under a 'logic' obeying the principle of what one might term its matrix intuition, that of the Εν διαφερον εαυτω, of the One differing from itself. This 'poetic logic', in Hölderlin's own terms, is the expression of the temporal dynamic and of the

original tearing apart, of the *Ur-teilung* of a totality that presents itself only in specific historical aspects. What appeared to me in reading the *Remarks on Sophocles* is the coincidence of the anti-rhythmic moment of caesura with that of speech, the concomitance of the suspension of the succession of representations and the appearance of the entirety of time under the figure of the divine, which implies that it is only in separation that the most intense intimacy with the totality [*le tout*] comes to pass and in human speech alone that the 'monstrous' and the sublime inhumanity of the world appears.

It was then, by taking from Heidegger himself the expression and the idea of a 'phenomenological chrono-logy', that I tried to outline in broad strokes the whole of the problem that had led me to question above all the texts of the philosophico-poetic trinity I had particularly chosen as my own: Husserl, Heidegger, Hölderlin. For what Heidegger understood in 1926 by chronology is certainly not the historical science of the same name but a discipline whose task is the investigation of the temporality of phenomena. It responds, in the period of the composition of *Being and Time*, to Heidegger's need at that time for a *Destruktion* of traditional logic and a development of a properly philosophical logic which would manage to reinsert in its own statements the temporal element, effaced in the process of formalisation, that would give back to αποφανσις its true sense of the *presentation* of phenomena. In this sense chrono-logy means therefore the

logic of temporality in opposition to traditional formal logic. But because the λογος in question here no longer has the formal sense it bears in the philosophical tradition, such a chronology can in no way be founded in the manner of an a priori science nor be assigned transcendental conditions of possibility. It can only in some way sketch itself inchoately *in actu* and exist only in its own attestation.

This is the reason why, no methodological treatise being possible in this regard, such a 'logic' of temporality can be improvised only in a joyous 'precipitation' opening onto no new architectonic, implying that, in a way, it no longer comes under 'philosophy' in a strict sense. It demands the *leap* into the event of presence and the taking into view of the, in principle, invisible or inapparent coming into presence of the present, while philosophy, in its 'evasive' transcendentalism, tries to reconstruct it the wrong way round, beginning with its result instead of setting itself up in becoming. It is this fundamental *anachronism* of the philosophical procedure that I have tried to bring to light by emphasising that it derives from the logicism inherent in the Western tradition which, since it has detached the apophantic statement from the existential and hermeneutic event whose result it is, has reified both speech and what is spoken of under the de-temporalising figure of *Vorhandenheit*, already accomplished presence. In this way, logic can be seen to be entirely derived from the 'ontology of pre-sence' whose existential sense is constituted by the denial of the finitude of existence.

Finally, I must emphasise that, on all these essential questions, and in particular on that of the privilege given to presence in the Western tradition, the work of Jacques Derrida has been for me, from the beginning, an extraordinary stimulation and that, like many others, I have remained, in large part moreover without his knowledge, constantly in *Gespräch* with him. However, I have never felt myself tied by what he himself has termed his 'positions', and what has been put forward as his 'thesis' of a logocentrism and phonocentrism characterising the whole of Western thought has always been for me, to borrow the exact words used by Heidegger in connection with Husserlian intentionality, not a 'password' [*mot de passe*] but 'the title of a central *problem*'.[4] For my part, I have been more tempted to see in the λογος, on condition that it is seen in its naissant moment and not in its result, the ek-centric element that opens the human ψυκη [the psyche], to all that it is not. The importance lent by the Western tradition, from its Indo-European roots, to the vivacity of speech and the breath of the voice has not seemed to me to be incompatible with the 'ek-centricity' Heidegger recognised in Dasein,[5] torn from the first by its temporality from self-presence.

In this taking up of Heideggerian questioning I have been concerned less to refute the Western tradition than to illuminate a question, that of time, since this tradition transmits the gift of its unthought[6] to us only to the extent that it remains for us a living tradition not reduced to dead material or doctrinal capital

whose management would then be the issue. It was such a *re-animation* of the tradition that Heidegger called *Destruktion*,[7] and I must admit that this enterprise of shaking academic culture has always found a profound echo in me.

For, doubtless like all those who, like me, were not born into the culture and, not feeling themselves to be its natural heirs, have had to acquaint themselves with it the hard way, I do not always feel at ease in the University and amongst those whom Jacques Taminiaux, in a very Hölderlinian manner, calls 'professional thinkers' – *die Berufsdenker*. This is why the relations I have maintained with philosophy, which since its Platonic beginnings has been inseparable from the educational institution, have at times been somewhat tense and why, far from feeling at home in philosophy, I have always been attracted to what Merleau-Ponty called its 'outside', which has taken for me the forms of poetry, drawing and orientalism. If, however, I have remained 'in' philosophy it is because I realised fairly early on that 'true' philosophy has no need of defence against contamination coming from outside since it is in reality, like the theology of the same name, a 'negative' philosophy which does not promote the positivity of any definitive truth, of any absolute order transcendent with respect to life, and which seeks rather to be the accomplishment of life *at the same time* as its reflexive taking up of itself, a thinking which is not Olympian, but a thinking of chiasmus. For, as Merleau-Ponty wrote in the notes

for one of his lectures rightly entitled 'Philosophy and Non-philosophy since Hegel' and given at the Collège de France in 1961, the year of his death and of my first reading of the *Phenomenology of Perception*:

> True philosophy laughs at philosophy, is a-philosophy.[8]

Notes

Abbreviations

Essays — *Friedrich Hölderlin: essays and letters on theory*, ed. and trans. Thomas Pfan (Albany, NY: SUNY Press, 1988)

GA — Martin Heidegger, the collected works (Gesamtausgabe)

UVS — W. von Humboldt, *Uber die Verschiedenheiten des menschlichen Sprachbaues und ihren Einfluss auf die geistige Entwicklung des Menschengeschlechts* (1830–5) from his collected works (Berlin: Behr, 1907), vol. 7

Prologue

tn Dire is translated sometimes with various forms of the verbs 'to tell' and 'to say'. For the sake of consistency, I have adopted the practice of modifying existing English translations of works quoted by the author, at times simply translating the French translation. Although references to English translations are given for the convenience of the reader, I have not always quoted them directly.

1. Heraclitus, Fragment 115 in the Diels-Kranz ordering. One must bear in mind that the word

ψυχη, which is related to the verb ψυχω (to breathe, respire), originally bore the sense of breath and subsequently came to mean breath of life, and soul.

2. Heraclitus, Fragment 45. I quote from Marcel Conche's translation, *Héraclite, Fragments* (Paris: P.U.F., 1986), p. 357: 'You will not find the limits of the soul, even travelling over every road, such is the depth of the discourse it holds.' I borrow from him the 'archaic word' *vastité* which he mentions in his commentary (*ibid.,* p. 359) in connection with the term βαθυς (deep).
3. Aristotle, *De Anima*, 417 b 5. This passage is repeatedly cited by Droysen to indicate that, in contrast with the uniformly repetitive course of nature, history is, on the contrary, characterised by a continuity of growth. Cf. H.-G. Gadamer, *Warheit und Method* (Tübingen: Mohr, 1960), p. 197; English-language edn, *Truth and Method*, trans. J. Weinsheimer and D. G. Marshall, 2nd rev. edn. (London: Sheed and Ward, 1989), p. 346.
4. Aristotle, *On Interpretation*, 16 a 20.
5. Cf. Heidegger, Gesamtausgabe, *Metaphysische Anfangsgründe der Logik im Ausgang von Leibniz*, vol. 26 (Gesamtausgabe volumes will henceforth be indicated by GA followed by the volume number) (Frankfurt am Main: Klostermann, 1978; the lecture course given in the summer semester of 1928), §12, p. 272; English-language edn, *The Metaphysical Foundations of Logic*, trans. Michael

Heim (Bloomington: Indiana University Press, 1984), p. 210, where the world is termed *nihil originarium* because, though not a being, it is nevertheless not a *nihil negativum*, an absolute nothing, either but is rather the nothing that temporalises itself originarily.

6. Cf. Parmenides, *Poem,* VIII, 60: 'the deployment of that which appears' following Jean Beaufret's translation in *Le poème de Parménide*, (Paris: P.U.F., 1955), p. 89.

1 THE IDEA OF A PHENOMENOLOGICAL CHRONO-LOGY

1. Nietzsche, *The Will to Power*, trans. Walter Kaufmann (London: Weidenfeld and Nicolson, 1967); *Nachgelassene Fragmente 1885–1887*, Critical Edition, vol. 12, ed. G. Colli and M. Montinari (Munich, Berlin and New York: de Gruyter, DTV, 1988), p. 104: '*Das Urteilen ist unser ältester Glaube, unser gewohntestes für-Wahr-oder für-Unwahrhalten ... Wenn ich sage "Der Blitz leuchtet", so habe ich das Leuchten einmal als Thätigkeit gesetzt und das andere Mal als Subjekt gesetzt: also zum Geschehen ein Sein supponiert, welches mit dem Geschehen nicht eins ist, vielmehr* ***bleibt, ist*** *und nicht "wird."*'
2. The terms 'activity' and 'articulation' that appear here refer to the Humboldtian conception of language, which constitutes not simply 'a' but 'the'

major reference of this 'sketch'. In opposition to the dominant tendency of modern linguistics, Humboldt saw immediately the essentially 'transitory' character of language whose definition can be only 'genetic'; see *Introduction à l'oeuvre sur le kavi* (1835; Paris: Seuil, 1974), p. 18. This is why he discovers the true 'grammar' of languages in the living activity of speech: '*Die Sprache liegt nur in der verbundenen Rede, Grammatik und Wörterbuch sind kaum ihren todten Gerippe vergleichbar*', *Über die Verschiedenheiten des menschlichen Sprachbaues* (1827–9), in *Gesammelte Schriften* (Collected Writings) (Berlin: Behr, 1907), vol. 6, 1, p. 147 ('Language is found only in the connection of discourse, grammar and dictionaries are barely comparable to its dead skeleton').

3. As M. Foucault remarks in his introduction to Arnauld and Lancelot's *Grammaire générale et raisonnée,* Grammaire de Port-Royal (Paris: Rep. Paulet, 1969): 'The sense of the word grammar is double: there is a grammar that is the immanent order of all spoken discourse and a grammar that is description, analysis and explanation – the theory of this order.' It is this 'immanent order', this syntax, that will progressively emerge into 'consciousness' (or, more precisely, be at the origin of what is so termed) and permit the development of the science of logic (επιστημη λογικη). It is true that theoretical grammar appeared in the Occident only in the Hellenistic epoch, but it in no way presup-

poses, as its name might wrongly lead us to believe, the fixing of spoken language in writing. One need only, in this respect, mention the work of Panini who around the fifth century BC, at an epoch in which writing was not yet a common tool for the notation of spoken language and in a fundamentally phonocentric tradition (that of the Veda), developed a meta-linguistic analysis of Sanskrit so perfect that today it still constitutes the most commonly used practical manual for learning this language. What the Greeks of Alexandria termed γραμματικη τεχνη, Panini termed *vyakarana*, a word that means at once manifestation and distinction, that is to say, analysis that renders visible and thus makes known the morphology and the syntax of spoken language. The project of the Port-Royal grammarians, that of a *general* grammar, has a far larger scope, as it aims to construct what could be termed a 'meta-grammar', an *a priori* grammar which resembles the 'logic of meaning' developed by Husserl in the fourth Logical Investigation. (Allow me, in this connection, to refer to my article 'Husserl and the Project of a Pure Logical Grammar' (1994), in the first issue of *Epreuves*.) In reality, as Heidegger emphasises in his doctoral thesis on Duns Scotus, this 'theory of the forms of meaning', brought back to prominence by Husserl, is in no way an invention of seventeenth-century rationalism. It already constituted the object of the medieval tradition of speculative grammar born in

the twelfth century, at the moment when an interest in Aristotelian dialectic awoke and when logical and grammatical studies were aiming to develop a critical analysis of thought founded on its grammatical expression and to construct a veritable 'logic of language'. The famous formula of the *Metalogicon* of John of Salisbury, ([which is] quoted by A. L. Kelkel in *La légende de l'être: Langage et poésie chez Heidegger* (Paris: Vrin, 1980), p. 40: '*Grammatica est totius philosophicae cunabulum*' ('Grammar is the cradle of all philosophy'), characteristic of this speculative turn in the science of grammar, could still serve as an epigraph to the work undertaken here.

4. B. Snell, *Die Entdeckung des Geistes* (Vandenhoek and Ruprecht, 1986), p. 205 ff.; English-language edn, *The Discovery of Mind*, trans. T. G. Rosenmeyer (Oxford: Blackwell, 1956), p. 227 ff. If B. Snell recognises in Greek culture, as many others before him have done, the source of the Enlightenment and the passage from 'μυθος' to 'λογος', myth to logos, this in no way implies that he considers Greece, as Classicism did, to be an a-historic model. On the contrary, he constantly emphasises the 'historical' aspect of the development of the notions of consciousness and thought, and the relative character of 'progress' implied by his thesis of a 'discovery' of the human spirit across the successive stages of epic, mythology, lyric poetry, tragedy and history.

5. Cf. Jean Beaufret, *Le poème de Parménide*, (Paris: P.U.F., 1955), p. 34 : 'But what then is the εον? In the end, is it not in this *participle* (μετοχη) that we have to experience how those traditional friends of the participle (φιλομετοχοι), the Greeks, were also, and perhaps because of this, true *friends of knowledge* (φιλοσοφιο)?'
6. I refer here to a course given by Paul Ricoeur in 1962–3 and circulated as a photocopy under the title 'Introduction au problème du signe, de la signification et du langage' ("Introduction to the problem of the sign, signification and language').
7. Aristotle, *On Interpretation*. That such an analysis, privileging the verb and not the noun, is possible in the field of Indo-European languages is shown by Panini's 'grammar' which rests on the principle of the verbal phrase whose centre is the verb and to which all the other factors of action (agent, instrument, object, etc.) are related in an equal manner. Cf. P. S. Filliozat, 'Les structures paninéennes' in *Le sanskrit* (Paris: P.U.F., Que sais-je?, 1992), p. 37 ff. See also what Humboldt says of the verb in general: 'it alone is assigned the act of *synthetic positing* as a grammatical function. . . . Between it and the other words of the simple sentence there is therefore a difference which forbids us to count it along with them in the same category', and of Sanskrit: 'In Sanskrit the indication of the verb's conjoining power rests solely on the grammatical treatment of this part of speech, and

since it follows the nature of the verb completely, there is absolutely nothing to complain of here. Since, on the point here in question, the verb in Sanskrit is by nature distinct from all other constituents of the simple sentence, it has nothing at all in common with the noun; the two remain perfectly pure and separate': Humboldt, *On Language: the diversity of human language structure and its influence on the mental development of mankind*, trans. Peter Heath (Cambridge: Cambridge University Press, 1988), pp. 185 and 186.

8. Aristotle, *On Interpretation*, III, 16 b 10. My emphasis.
9. *Ibid.*, III, 16 b 20.
10. *Ibid.*, II, 16 a 20.
11. *Ibid.*, III, 16 b 6.
12. *Ibid.*, III, 16 b 12–19.
13. This point has been particularly well brought out by Johannes Lohmann in *Philosophie und Sprachwissenschaft* ('Philosophy and Linguistics') (Berlin: Dunker und Humblot, 1965), p. 176 ff. He speaks on this subject, and I think rightly so, of the beginning with Aristotle of a 'logicisation of time' which reaches completion in 'Enlightenment' Europe with the de-temporalisation (*Entzeitlichung*) of the Latin *ratio* become 'reason' (*op. cit.*, p. 252).
14. Inflection has, since the publication in 1808 of Friedrich Schlegel's famous book, *Uber die Sprache und Weisheit der Indier* ('*On the Language and*

Wisdom of the Indians'), been a criterion which has allowed a classification of languages to be developed. Humboldt for his part refused to make of it a line of absolute demarcation between languages ('*In keiner Sprache ist Alles Beugung, in keiner Alles Anfügung*', *Gesammelte Schriften*, vol. 6, 1, *op. cit.*, p. 275: 'In no language is everything inflection, in no language is everything agglutination'). Every language can thus be understood on the basis of the idea of inflection, even when this is not marked as in the case of Chinese, which, as opposed to Sanskrit, a language in which inflection is very marked, assigns to position and not the phonetic the task of expressing grammatical form. This calls for 'a high degree of internal tension' and does not therefore allow Chinese to be considered an inferior form of language (*On Language*, *op. cit.*, p. 280). Nevertheless, one must note that Panini's 'analysis' had already, at around 500 BC, distinguished the radical from the ending and had thus illuminated the characteristic of inflection proper to Indo-European languages. Semitic languages are distinct from the latter as their inflection concerns a root which – contrary to the Indo-European radical which is merely a product of analysis and becomes apparent only through etymological research – is part of the living linguistic consciousness of the speaker without, however, ever being embodied otherwise than in consonantal script.

15. Aristotle, *On Interpretation*, II, 16 b 1 and III, 16 b 17. See also Aristotle, *Poetics*, 1457 a 18.
16. Heidegger, *Einführung in die Metaphysik* (Tübingen: Niemeyer, 1966), p. 46; English-language end, *An Introduction to Metaphysics*, trans. Ralph Manheim (New Haven, CT and London: Yale University Press, 1959), pp. 59–60.
17. Cf. J. Lohmann, 'Das Verhältnis des abendländischen Menschen zur Sprache' ("The Relationship of Western Peoples to Language") in *Lexis*, vol. 3, 1, 1952, p. 39. One must emphasise here the importance of the concept of στερησις (privation or non-form) that Aristotle constructs in order to allow contraries to meet in the third term – the substrate (υποκειμενον) (*Metaphysics* Λ, 10, 1075 a 30). Every transformation taking place in the world thus finds itself explained as the movement between a form (μορφη) and the non-form (στερησις) corresponding in a substrate (υλη as υποκειμενον).
18. Heidegger, *Logik. Die Frage nach der Wahrheit* ("Logic. The Question of Truth") (Frankfurt am Main: Klostermann, 1976), GA 21, p. 160. A little earlier (p. 157) Heidegger mentions an example of a proposition often quoted within the field of traditional logic: 'The roses are blooming'. As a determinate judgement, it means that those things that are the roses have the property of blooming and not that the roses are blooming *presently*, which, however, is what anyone who uttered such a phrase would mean.

19. *Ibid.*, p. 161.
20. *Ibid.*, p. 163 ff. The passages cited by Heidegger are *Metaphysics*, Γ 7, 1011 b 26 and E, 4, 1027 b 20–2.
21. Cf. GA 21, p. 142, where Heidegger emphasises that Aristotle 'was not able to free himself from the orientation by way of language – an impossibility for the Greeks'. It is here in §12 that Heidegger draws the distinction for the first time between the hermeneutic-comprehensive 'as' and its apophantic-determinate modification which forms the fundamental structure of §32 and §33 of *Sein und Zeit*, (Tübingen: Niemeyer, 1953); English-language edn, *Being and Time*, trans. J. Stambaugh (Albany, NY: SUNY Press, 1996). See the third chapter of this sketch ('Logic and Metaphysics').
22. *Ibid.*, p. 164.
23. *Ibid.*, p. 168.
24. *Ibid.*, pp. 170–82. In these pages Heidegger offers a translation of and commentary on this chapter.
25. It is important to emphasise, as Heidegger does, that Aristotle specifies that this αγνοειν is not a pure blindness, that is to say, a pure absence of thought (νοειν), as there is here also a λεγειν, the grasping that permits enunciation (φασις). Therefore, what is uniquely not possible here is διανοιεν and διαλεγεσθαι, thought and determinative discourse, which suppose the reciprocity of συνθεσις and διαιρεσις.

26. GA 21, p. 135.
27. *Ibid.*, p. 197: as the title of §15 announces.
28. *Ibid.*, p. 199.
29. *Ibid.*, p. 200.
30. *Ibid.*
31. *Ibid.*, pp. 204–5.
32. To bring this into play, Heidegger quotes here in §15 one of Kant's *Reflections*, which says: '*Der Philosophen Geschäft ist nicht, Regeln zu geben, sondern die geheimen Urteile der gemeinen Vernunft zu zergliedern*' ('The business of philosophy does not consist in giving rules, but in analysing the secret judgements of the common reason'). Heidegger sees in the latter 'those ways of conducting oneself which, unformulated, unknown and not understood, are at the basis of Dasein's everyday comportments' (*op. cit.*, p. 197).
33. *Ibid.*, p. 201. Note that it is at this same period (1926) that Heidegger receives from Husserl the manuscript of *On the Phenomenology of the Consciousness of Internal Time*, which is another attempt, besides Kant's, to plunge into the 'hyletic' depths of consciousness and to think this intimacy with time. Heidegger, who published the manuscript he had received only in 1928, had nevertheless continued to accord to Kant the exclusive privilege of an approach to the temporality of being, as the *Kantbook* of 1929 attests.
34. *Ibid.*, p. 11.
35. *Ibid.*, p. 13.

36. *Ibid.*, p. 15.
37. *Ibid.*: '*Denken und gar wissenschaftliches Denken ist nur zu lernen im Umgang mit den Sachen.*'
38. *Ibid.*, pp. 18–19. This relationship, itself philosophical, to the philosophical content still alive in the historic sediment recalls the Hegelian conception of the relation of philosophy to its own history, as Hegel expressed it in this famous sentence from his first publication: '*Der lebendige Geist, der in einer Philosophie wohnt, verlangt, um sich zu enthüllen, durch einen verwandten Geist geboren zu werden*', *Differenzschrift* in *Hegel Werke, Jeaner Schriften 1801–1807*, (Frankfurt am Main: Suhrkamp, 1970), vol. 2, p. 16 ('To reveal itself, the living spirit that inhabits a philosophy demands the affinity of a spirit that brings it into the world').
39. *Ibid*., p. 18.
40. It is Husserl who affirms in the introduction to the *Logical Investigations*, trans. J. N. Findlay (London: Routledge, 1970), vol. 1, Introduction, §2, p. 250, that the 'objects which pure logic seeks to examine are, in the first instance, therefore given to it in grammatical clothing (*im grammatichen Gewande*)'. It becomes clear here that the Husserlian concept of the 'lived experience' (*Erlebnis*), as well as the theory of logical signification that he develops in the *Investigations*, presupposes the 'naturalisation' at the origin of psychological science. Heidegger declares that 'it

was their good fortune that the Greeks had no "lived experiences" ' in *Nietzsche I* (Pfullingen: Neske, 1961), p. 95; English-language edn, *Nietzsche*, trans. D. F. Krell (New York: Harper and Row, 1979), p. 80; when he does so he refers not only to the absence amongst them of aesthetics and psychology but also to the fact that they 'lived' so profoundly in words, as Husserl would say, that they never differentiated their 'mental processes' from their verbal expressions, thus manifesting the fundamental historicality that Heidegger terms no longer 'life' but rather existence. This then is what is most proper to human existence: that it is so originarily structured by language that it can no longer appear to itself as 'nature'.

41. I take the liberty of referring here to p. 108 ff. of my book *Heidegger et la question de temps* ("Heidegger and the Question of Time") (Paris: P.U.F., 1990).

42. This is what Heidegger himself said explicitly in 1949: ' *"Sein" ist in "Sein und Zeit" nicht etwas anderes als "Zeit", insofern der "Zeit" als der Vornahme für die Wahrheit des Seins genannt wird, welche Wahrheit das Wesende des Seins und so das Sein selbst ist.*' See ' "Being" in "*Being and Time*" is nothing other than "time", insofar as "time" is given as the fore-name [*pré-nom, Vornahme*] of the truth of being, which truth is the essence of being and so being itself.') (*Was ist Metaphysik*, (Frankfurt am Main: Klostermann, 1960), p. 17.

43. Cf. *Beiträge zur Philosophie* ("Contributions to Philosophy") (Frankfurt am Main: Klostermann, 1989), pp. 191–2, where it is clearly stated that time, thought of as temporalisation (*Zeitung*), ecstatic rapture (*Entrückung*) and openness (*Eröffnung*), is at the same time what institutes space (*einräumend*), creating space, that 'is not even of the same essence as it, but belongs to it just as it (time) belongs to space'; see also §238 and §242 gathered under the title 'Der Zeitraum als Ab-grund' ('Space-time as Abyss'), p. 371 ff.
44. Cf. *On Time and Being*, trans. Joan Stambaugh (New York: Harper, 1972) , p. 14 and the French translator's note in *Questions IV* (Paris: Gallimard, 1976) p. 50: 'The free space of time (*Zeit-Raum*) has nothing to do with the physicist's space-time. The latter is a parameter for a still more mathematical calculation. Heidegger's *Zeit-Raum*, on the other hand, is the unity of a state of openness which is the place not only of time and its ecstatic temporalisation but also of space and its spacing. *Zeit-Raum* could almost be translated as "spacing of time".' See, *Questions IV*, p. 133; *On Time and Being*, p. 69.
45. See, for example, the Le Thor seminar (1969) in *Questions IV*, *op. cit.*, p. 278.
46. See 'Mein Weg in die Phänomenologie' in *Zur Sache des Denkens* (Pfullingen: Neske, 1969), p. 90; English-language trans., 'My Way to Phenomenology' in *On Time and Being*, *op. cit.*,

p. 82, where Heidegger defines phenomenology as 'the possibility of thinking, at times changing and only thus persisting, of corresponding to the claim of what is to be thought' and where he emphasises that if it is experienced and retained in this way it could then disappear as a designation (*Titel*) 'in favour of the *Sache des Denkens* (task of thinking) whose manifestness remains a mystery'. The disappearance here of the 'designation', which like any 'rubric' refers to a possible 'architectonic' and to the scholarly edifice of science, in itself manifests the placing of thought at the service of the 'thing itself', which is no longer thought as being able to be fully exhibited in knowledge of the self. See in the following chapter what is said of the 'phenomenology of the inapparent'.

47. Cf. H.-G. Gadamer, *Truth and Method*, trans. J. Weinsheimer and D. G. Marshall, 2nd rev. edn. (London: Sheed and Ward, 1989), p. 346: 'The aim of science is so to objectify experience that it no longer contains any historical (*geschichtlich*) element. Scientific experiment does this through its methodical procedure. The historico-critical method, however, does something similar in the human sciences. Through the objectivity of their approach, both methods are concerned to guarantee that these basic experiences can be repeated by anyone. Just as in the natural sciences experiments must be verifiable, so also must the whole process be capable of being checked in the human sciences

also. Hence there can be no place for the historicity of experience in science.' This passage is recalled by Johannes Lohmann in *Philosophie und Sprachwissenschaft*, *op. cit.*, p. 178, at the moment when, having defined his own project as that of the constitution of a semantic logic in opposition to the structuralist's logic of designation (*op. cit.,* p. 155), he shows that this project involves re-introducing the temporal moment into traditional logic, itself defined as the limit form of a universal meta-language issuing from the general structure of the human 'language game' of the 'something as something' (*etwas-als-etwas-Struktur*). This limit form or zero point of the semantic relation is that of the 'plain' equivalence of words and things in what could be called the 'picture theory' of language, from which is missing the 'tension' that flows from the relation to the *actuality* of what is spoken about and to the process of a temporality whose occurrence is *underway* [*en train de se faire*].

48. Heidegger, *Aus der Erfahrung des Denkens* ("From the Experience of Thinking"), 2nd edn. (Pfullingen: Neske, 1965), p. 23.
49. Heidegger, *Basic Writings*, 2nd rev. edn, ed. D. F. Krell (New York: HarperCollins, 1993), p. 217.
50. Heidegger, 'Logos' (1951) in *Early Greek Thinking*, trans. D. F. Krell and F. A. Capuzzi (New York: HarperCollins, 1974), p. 78.
51. This, for certainly different though not incomparable reasons, was already the problem for what

could only absurdly call itself 'grammatology', whose conditions of impossibility were demonstrated – in a still negatively transcendental sense – in *Of Grammatology* whose very last sentence, at the very least, must be quoted here: 'Grammato*logy*, this thought would still remain enclosed in presence'; J. Derrida, *De la grammatologie* (Paris: Ed. de Minuit, 1967), p. 142; English-language edn, *Of Grammatology*, trans. Gayatri Chakravorty Spivak (Baltimore,, MD: Johns Hopkins University Press, 1976), p. 93.

52. Cf. Merleau-Ponty, *Phénoménologie de la perception* (Paris: Gallimard, 1945), Avant-Propos, p. xv English-language edn, *Phenomenology of Perception*, trans. Colin Smith (London: Routledge, 1962), preface, p. xxi.
53. The term *esquisse* doubtless comes through the Italian *schizzo* from the Latin *schedium* (improvised poem, impromptu) and relates in Greek to the adjective σχεδιος: "hastily done, improvised, of the moment", to the adverbs σχεδιην: 'nearby, in the field', and σχεδιως: 'hastily, lightly, negligently, vainly', and to the substantive *scedia*, designating any light and hastily built construction. That living might consist in preparing oneself, from the most tender childhood to the most extreme old age, for a few instants of successful improvisation, could doubtless be truly understood only in an explicitly 'phonocentric' tradition such as the Indian tradition in which music and poetry have remained closely

tied and are still considered to be two similar modes of expression. The musician, like the poet required to write a sonnet or an ode, has imposed upon him the form and structure of the *raga* which he is going to improvise. This aspect of the tradition of the *raga* is no less important than the ancestral theory that determines, in accordance with the time of day chosen for the improvisation, the imposed form of the sequence of notes with predetermined interrelations that comprises the *raga*, whose name, outside of its technical sense of a musical mode, means red, the colour of passion, and the charm of the voice. I refer here not to works of musicology but to the enlightened judgement expressed in his memoirs by Yehudi Menuhin, one of the rare Western interpreters to attempt the art of improvisation in which Indian music consists. See his *Unfinished Journey* (London: Futura Publications, 1978), p. 339 ff.

54. Kant, *Critique of Pure Reason*, trans. Norman Kemp Smith (London: Macmillan, 1929), p. 47.
55. See René Char, 'Le Poème pulvérisé', XXIV, in *Oeuvres complètes*, (Paris: Gallimard, Pléiade, 1983), p. 266: 'If we dwell in a lightning flash, it is the heart of the eternal.'

2 Phenomenology and Temporality

1. '*Während eine Bewegung wahrgenommen wird, findet Moment für Moment ein Als "Jetzt" Erfassen*

statt, darin konstituiert sich die jetzt aktuelle Phase der Bewegung selbst. Aber diese Jetzt-Auffassung ist gleichsam der Kern zu einem Kometenschweif von Retentionen, auf die früheren Jetztpunkte der Bewegung bezogen.' See *On The Phenomenology of the Consciousness of Internal Time (1893–1917)*, trans. John Barnett Brough (Dordrecht: Kluwer, 1991), §11, p. 32.
2. GA 21, p. 200.
3. Husserl, *The Idea of Phenomenology*, trans. W. P. Alston and G. Nakhnikian (The Hague: Nijhoff, 1964), p. 19.
4. 'Epilogue' in Husserl, *Ideas Pertaining to a Pure Phenomenology and to Phenomenological Philosophy*, book 2, trans. R. Rojcewicz and A. Schuwer (Dordrecht: Kluwer, 1989), p. 406.
5. *Ibid.* Note, once and for all, that the traditional translation of the German *streng* as 'rigorous' rather than 'strict' has resulted, in this case as in many others, in what Jacques Derrida has called 'the effacement of language'; (see his *Parages* (Paris: Galilée, 1986), p. 139 ff. What Latin languages understand as rigidity, inflexibility, hardness – and all *rigour* is nothing less than a rigor mortis – Germanic languages understand rather as force (*streng,* which is the same word as the English 'strong', and which is related to the Greek στραγγος and to the Latin *stringere*, bears the sense of 'tightened', 'tensed'). The rigorous science in which, for Husserl, philosophy consists is rigorous

not by virtue of a rigid and frozen character but uniquely because it has the strength to found itself, to be, as Kant also said, the '*Selbsthalterin*', 'the guardian' of its own laws, but in the sense that it itself constitutes their unique support; see his *Groundwork for the Metaphysics of Morals* (Indianapolis: Hackett, 1981), p. 34.

6. Husserl, in emphasising the self-foundational (*Wissenschaft aus letzter Begründung*) and ultimately self-responsible (*aus letzter Selbst-verantwortung*) character of philosophy ('Epilogue' to the *Ideas*, *op. cit.*; see Husserliana, vol. 5, 1952, p. 139, trans. p. 406), remained within the lineage of German Idealism, which, since Kant, had viewed philosophy as the 'science' of freedom. Cf. Hegel, *Encyclopedia of Philosophical Sciences*, 1817 Introduction, §5, 'Philosophy can be considered the science of freedom, because in it the alien character of ob-jects disappears and, through this, the finitude of consciousness; it is uniquely in it that contingency, natural necessity and the relation to exteriority in general disappear and, through this, dependence, nostalgia and fear: it is only in philosophy that reason is absolutely with itself [*auprés d'elle-même*].'
7. See the famous passage from the *Sophist* (244a) quoted as an epigraph to *Sein und Zeit*, which speaks of the confusion that reigned from Parmenides to Plato over the meaning, become obscure, of the word ον.

8. For all that concerns the constitution of school metaphysics and the origin of the word 'ontology', see J.-F. Courtine's remarkable work devoted to *Suarez et le système de la metaphysique* ("Suarez and the System of Metaphysics") (Paris: P.U.F., 1990), in particular pp. 248 to 263.
9. Cf. Beaufret, *Le poème de Parménide* (Paris: P.U.F., 1955), p. 48, who opposes 'the evasive transcendence which, since Plato, is metaphysically ours' to 'a founding transcendence' which is nowhere more striking than in Parmenides's *Poem*, whose place is that of 'being in the greatest intimacy of *Difference* which has carried as far as us the more and more latent ambiguity of the word εον', a difference according to which 'it is in the greatest intimacy of εον [being] that δοκουντα [appearances] are "born", it is in the greatest intimacy of αληθεια [truth] that the origin and necessity of δοξα [opinion] is located'. What Jean Beaufret calls 'being in the greatest intimacy of *Difference*' is to be thought here as a transcendence that, in its lightning flash, bursts forth in immanence itself, tearing it apart in order to make it appear.
10. Cf. Nietzsche, *On the Genealogy of Morals*, third essay (Cambridge: Cambridge University Press, 1994), where, having emphasised that the '*bête philosophique*' (philosophical creature) seeks the conditions favourable to independence in the ascetic ideal (§7) and that without this ascetic misconception of itself philosophy would not have

been possible on earth, Nietzsche poses the question: 'Is there enough pride, daring, courage, self-confidence, will of spirit, will to take responsibility, *freedom of will*, for "the philosopher" on earth to be really – *possible*?' (§10). One might very well, with Heidegger, think this true freedom of will, not as 'will to power', which is to say 'will to will', but as *Gelassenheit* (releasement) and as letting-be.

11. Cf. G. Granel, *L'équivoque ontologique de la pensée kantienne* ("The Ontological Equivocation of Kantian Thought") (Paris: Gallimard, 1970), p. 60 ff.
12. This point, which for Husserl amounts to showing that Kant was, from the first, unfaithful to his call to finitude in leaving intact within his critical philosophy a core of classical infinitism, was particularly well set out in the unpublished course given by Jacques Derrida at the Sorbonne in 1962–3 (second semester) on 'Phenomenology, theology and teleology in Husserl'. It is true that he mentioned equally Kant's possible response to Husserl, which would accuse him also of forgetting finitude, which can ever be given only against the horizon of the infinite.
13. In connection with a possible placing in relation of Nietzsche and Husserl, permit me to refer to my articles 'Réduction et intersubjectivité' ("Reduction and Inter-subjectivity") in *Husserl*, collection published under the direction of E. Escoubas and M.

Richir (Grenoble: Millon, 1988), p. 54 and 'Husserl et la neutralité de l'art' ("Husserl and the Neutrality of Art") published in *La Part de l'Oeil* (Brussels: 1991), p. 19 ff.

14. See, in this regard, my article 'Réduction et inter-subjectivité', *op. cit.*, p. 43 ff.
15. Cf. *Cartesian Meditations* (The Hague: Nijhoff, 1950), §41, p. 86: 'Only someone who misunderstands either the deepest sense of intentional method, or that of transcendental reduction, or perhaps both, can attempt to separate phenomenology from transcendental idealism.'
16. Let us merely allude to them here: for Plato, besides the myth in the *Phaedrus* and the allegory of the cave, whose topology relates to the duality of sensible and intelligible worlds, the criticisms that he addresses to himself in the *Parmenides* under the name 'the third man argument' and that are applicable, precisely, to a topical and spatialising understanding of μετεξις [participation], which is doubtless that of common opinion and not that of the philosopher; for Kant, the uniting of transcendental idealism with empirical realism, proceeding from the explicit distinction between appearance (*Schein*) and phenomenon (*Erscheinung*), the latter itself being, as one of the reflections of the *Opus Postumum* attests, the *same* object as the thing in itself, though considered from the perspective of another *intuitus*; finally, for Hegel, even though he is not taken into consideration by Nietzsche, the idea,

already forcefully expressed in the second chapter of the *Phenomenology of Spirit*, that the super-sensible world, which is merely the inversion of the sensible world, must be thought as being substantially one with the latter, to which it is opposed only in a representation that might be termed *eikastic*.

17. Cf. Husserl, *Ideas*, trans. W. R. Boyce Gibson (London: Allen and Unwin, 1931), p. 86: 'If by "*Positivism*" we are to mean the absolute unbiased grounding of all science on what is "positive", i.e., on what can be primordially apprehended, then it is *we* who are the genuine positivists.'
18. Cf. the manuscript from 1934 bearing the title 'Reversal of the Copernican Doctrine' of which a French translation by Didier Franck has been published in *Le terre ne se meut pas* ("The Earth Does Not Move") (Paris: Ed. de Minuit, 1989), pp. 11–29. This text's anti-Copernican move can be understood as an obstinate fidelity to the sense of *Fundierung* presented in the *Logical Investigations* and as a refusal of the perfecting of the Kantian 'Copernican revolution' in which absolute idealism consists, and which celebrates the triumph of what Husserl considers to be the myth of the spontaneity of an understanding completely detached from the receptivity of sensibility.
19. Fragment 60 in the Diels-Kranz ordering.
20. Cf. Husserl, *Logical Investigations*, trans. J. N. Findlay (London: Routledge, 1970), book 3, investigation 6, §48 to §52. If we consider an example

often invoked by Husserl, that of the categorial perception of the *species* red, it is clear that it is this eidetic intuition that makes possible the perception of this singular red *as* red. However, it is this singular perception that is the foundation, but not the content, of the eidetic intuition which does not aim at the singular perception itself though constructing itself on it, whilst, for example, in the act of conjunction, which is a synthetic act, a singular perception is taken up as the content of the new categorial objectivity of the form 'S is P *and* Q'.

21. Heidegger, *Prolegomena zur Geschichte des Zeitbegriffs*, GA 20 (Frankfurt am Main: Klostermann, 1979), p. 94; English-language edn, *History of the Concept of Time*, trans. Theodore Kisiel (Bloomington: Indiana University Press, 1985), p. 69.
22. Aristotle, *De Anima*, 431 a.
23. Cf. *Logical Investigations*, book 3, *op. cit.*, §44, p. 784. Husserl here sets the imagination on the same plane as perception in affirming that a concept 'can only "arise", i.e., become *self-given* to us, if based on an act which at least sets some individual instance of it before our eyes, *if only imaginatively*' (my italics).
24. GA 20, p. 96/70. Cf. *Logical Investigations*, book 3, *op. cit.*, p. 801 ff.
25. GA 20, p. 98/72.
26. Cf. John Sallis, *Delimitations Phenomenology and*

the End of Metaphysics, 2nd rev. edn. (Bloomington: Indiana University Press, 1995), p. 27. A note refers to an earlier book by the same author, *The Gathering of Reason* (Columbus: Ohio University Press, 1980), entirely devoted to Kant's philosophy, where the same idea is expressed: 'This turning away from the traditional distinction between the sensible and the intelligible has the character of an *Aufhebung* [sublation], for the distinction is unsuppressible, already re-invoked with the very speech that would banish it. It is a matter of reopening that distinction within the new conception of the sensible – or rather, a matter of establishing it, for in the assimilation of pure thought to sensible experience, the distinction has already been brought back into play within this new dimension' (*op. cit.*, p. 171).

27. Cf. Kant, *Critique of Pure Reason*, trans. Norman Kemp Smith (London: Macmillan, 1929), Introduction, 3, A5, p. 47.
28. Cf. Husserl, *Experience and Judgement*, trans. James S. Churchill and Karl Ameriks (London: Routledge, 1973), §65, p. 267. See in this connection, Jacques Derrida, *L'origine de la géométrie* (Paris: P.U.F., 1962), p. 63 ff; English-language edn, *The Origin of Geometry*, trans. John P. Leavey (Lincoln: University of Nebraska Press, 1978), p. 72.
29. *Ibid.*, p. 261.
30. Much has been said, in relation to Husserl, about an

'idealist turn' coinciding with the discovery of the phenomenological reduction and superseding the 'neutrality', from the metaphysical point of view, or even the 'realism' of the *Logical Investigations*. If there is a 'turn', it seems to me that this could only be *within* an idealism indistinguishable from philosophy itself and that this turn could have only the sense of the rendering limitless of the phenomenal field since it leads to a subjectivisation of the phenomenon and to an identification of egology and ontology.

31. Cf. Schelling, *Idées pour une philosophie de la nature* ("Ideas for a Philosophy of Nature") (Appendix) in *Essais* (Paris: Aubier Montaigne, 1946), p. 97.
32. *Sein und Zeit* (Tübingen: Niemeyer, 1953), p. 208; English-language edn, *Being and Time*, trans. J. Stambaugh (Albany, NY: SUNY Press,).
33. *Ibid*.
34. A marginal note in the '*Huttenexemplar*' (the copy of *Sein und Zeit* annotated by Heidegger in his 'cabin' in Todnauberg from 1927) next to the phrase which says (*op. cit*., p. 208) that 'being can never be explained by beings' recognises here the 'ontological difference'.
35. Cf. Heidegger, *The Basic Problems of Phenomenology* (the course given in the summer of 1927), trans. Albert Hofstadter (Bloomington: Indiana University Press, 1982), §5, p. 19 ff. For his part Heidegger understands the reduction as

leading vision back from beings to being (*op. cit.*, p. 21).

36. Cf. *Ideas*, *op. cit.*, §31, p. 107, the paragraph in which Husserl defines the 'natural thesis' on the basis of the character of presence ('*Character "da", "vorhanden"*') attributed pre-predicatively to anything perceived.
37. Cf. Heidegger, 'The End of Philosophy and the Task of Thinking' in *On Time and Being*, trans. Joan Stambaugh (New York: Harper, 1972), pp. 65–6, where Heidegger quotes this reflection of Goethe's.
38. *Sein und Zeit*, *op. cit.*, p. 36.
39. *Ibid.*
40. *The Idea of Phenomenology*, *op. cit.*, p. 10.
41. *Ibid.*
42. *Ibid.*
43. GA 20, p. 97/71. A passage from a letter of Husserl's to Hocking of 25 January 1903, quoted by W. Biemel in 'Les phases décisives de la développement de la pensée de Husserl' ('The Decisive Phases of the Development of Husserl's Thought'), *Husserl*, Cahiers de Royaumont, Philosophie 3 (Paris: Ed. de Minuit, 1959), p. 46, is in the same vein: 'The expression which returns so many times, that "objects" "constitute" themselves in an act, always designates the propriety of the act of *making the object representable*; it is not a question of "constituting" in the literal sense.'
44. *Ibid.*, p. 116. In this way, one can rebut the simplification, too often presented as 'obvious', particularly

in France, which consists in viewing Husserl as a Cartesian, whilst phenomenology, even and above all in its 'transcendental' version, demands the overcoming of Cartesianism, which is to say, the overcoming of the enclosure within the subjective sphere of the 'indubitable given', for which Husserl explicitly calls in his course of 1911. See Husserl, *Les problèmes fondamentaux de la phenomenologie* ("The Fundamental Problems of Phenomenology") (Paris: P.U.F., 1991), chapter 4, p. 159 ff.

45. Cf. *Sein und Zeit*, *op. cit.*, p. 15: 'The kind of being which belongs to Dasein is rather such that, in understanding its own being, it has a tendency to do so in terms of that being towards which it comports itself proximally and in a way which is essentially constant – in terms of the "world".'
46. *Ideas*, *op. cit.*, §85, p. 246.
47. *Ibid.*, §49, p. 153.
48. *Ibid.*, §81, p. 236.
49. *Ibid.*, note to p. 236.
50. Cf. Gérard Granel, *Le sens du temps et de la perception chez E. Husserl* ("The Sense of Time and Perception in E. Husserl") (Paris: Gallimard, 1968), p. 45 ff. This 'intimacy' of a temporality and a consciousness 'which manage to remain in each other' is understood not as 'psychological interiority' but as the very intimacy of the Absolute.
51. *Ibid.*, p. 73.
52. *On the Phenomenology of the Consciousness of Internal Time*, *op. cit.*, §39, p. 84 ff.

53. *Ibid*., p. 88. Allow me to refer in this regard to my article 'Le temps et l'autre chez Husserl et Heidegger' ("Time and the Other in Husserl and Heidegger") published in *Alter*, 1, 1993, p. 385 ff.
54. Cf. Kant, *Critique of Pure Reason*, *op. cit*., B180–1: 'This schematism of our understanding, in its application to appearances and their mere form, is an art concealed in the depths of the human soul, whose real modes of activity (*Handgriffe*) nature is hardly likely ever to allow us to discover, and *to have open to our gaze* (*sie unverdeckt vor Augen legen*)' (my italics). See in this regard the analysis Paul Ricoeur devotes to the Kantian thesis of the invisibility of time in *Time and Narrative*, vol. 3, trans. Kathleen Blamey and David Pellauer (Chicago: University of Chicago Press, 1988), p. 44 ff.
55. Cf. Granel, *Le sens du temp, op. cit*., p. 47, from which I am drawing here, in its broad outlines, the remarkable interpretation of Husserl's lectures on the phenomenology of the consciousness of internal time, of 1905, an interpretation that, as he himself emphasises (p. 113), consists in reading Husserl to show how his ultimate questions call for the Heideggerian renewal without, however, establishing themselves in the Heideggerian 'site'.
56. *Ibid*., p. 73, where it is noted that Husserl returns in this way 'to the fundamental idea that philosophy in its Kantian moment had inherited something from its Cartesian moment, namely that being does not affect us'.

57. *On the Phenomenology of the Consciousness of Internal Time*, *op. cit.*, §6, p. 16.
58. *Ibid.,* §16, p. 40/42. This passage is quoted by Granel (*Le sens du temp*, *op. cit.*, p. 82) and is compared with the analysis in §143 of *Ideas* I where, at the level of the 'provisional' absolute of noetic phenomenology, 'the perfect given of the thing is stipulated *as Idea* (in the Kantian sense)', whilst, at the level of the 'definitive' absolute of hyletic phenomenology, it no longer appears as a stipulated external limit but as the internal τελος (end) which is also the αρχη (origin) of a living continuum from which nothing 'detaches' itself.
59. Granel (*Le sens du temp, op. cit.*, p. 84) takes the expression 'comet's tail', used by Husserl in §11 of *On the Phenomenology of the Consciousness of Internal Time*, in this sense.
60. *Ibid.*, I refer here to the dazzling descriptions of p. 86 ff.
61. Cf. Henri Bergson, 'La perception du changement', *La pensée et le mouvant*, in *Oeuvres*, (Paris: P.U.F., 1963), p. 1381 ff.; English-language edn, 'Perception of change' in *A Study in Metaphysics: the Creative Mind* (Totowa, NJ: Littlefield, Adams, 1965), p. 150.
62. *On the Phenomenology of the Consciousness of Internal Time*, *op. cit*., p. 74/78.
63. *Ibid.*, p. 75/79.
64. Merleau-Ponty, *Le visible et l'invisible* (Paris: Gallimard, 1964), pp. 282–3, English-language edn, *The Visible and the Invisible*, trans. Alphonso

Lingis (Evanston, IL: Northwestern University Press, 1968), p. 229: 'The invisible is *there* without being an *object*, it is pure transcendence, without an ontic masque.'

65. 'Time and Being' in *On Time and Being*, *op. cit.*, p. 19, 'What determines both, time and being, in their own, that is, in their belonging together, we shall call: *Ereignis*.'
66. *Ibid.*, p. 2.
67. Cf. Heidegger, 'Letter on Humanism' in *Basic Writings*, 2nd rev. edn, ed. D. F. Krell (New York: HarperCollins, 1993), p. 223; 'But if man is to find his way once again into the nearness of being he must first learn to exist in the nameless [*im Namenlosen*].'
68. Granel, *Le sens du temp, op. cit.*, p. 99.
69. *Ibid.*, p. 112.
70. *Ibid.*
71. *Ibid.*, p. 120.
72. *Sein und Zeit*, *op. cit.*, p. 25: '*eine echte philosophische Verlegenheit*'.
73. Cf. *On Time and Being*, *op. cit.*, p. 4 [*Zur Sache des Denkens* (Pfullingen: Neske, 1969), p. 4; English-language trans., 'My Way to Phenomenology' in *On Time and Being*].
74. *Ibid.*, p. 23/23.
75. *Ibid.*, p. 24/24 : '*Das Ereignis* ist *weder, noch* gibt *es das Ereignis. Das Eine wie das Andere sagen, bedeutet eine Verkehrung des Sachverhalts, gleich als wollten wir den Quell aus dem Strom herleiten*.'

76. Cf. the Zähringen seminar (1973) in *Questions IV* (Paris: Gallimard, 1976), p. 339.
77. *Ibid.*, p. 336 ff.
78. *Unscheinbar* can be rendered in French not only literally by *inapparent* but also by *insignifiant* [insignificant] in the sense of 'what passes unnoticed' for want of brightness and consequently does not attract attention.
79. *The Visible and The invisible*, *op. cit.*, p. 229.
80. *Sein und Zeit*, *op. cit.*, p. 222
81. Cf. 'The Origin of the Work of Art' in *Basic Writings*, *op. cit.*, p. 179: 'This means that the open place in the midst of beings, the clearing, is never a rigid stage with a permanently raised curtain on which the play of beings runs its course. . . . The unconcealment of beings (*Unverborgenheit des Seienden*) – this is never a merely existent state (*ein nur vorhandener Zustand*), but an event.'
82. Cf. Heidegger, 'The Thing' in *Poetry, Language, Thought*, trans. Albert Hofstadter (New York: Harper and Row, 1971), pp. 181–2.
83. *Ibid.*, p. 174 ff.
84. *Ibid.*, p. 182. Cf. *Vorträge und Aufsätze* (Pfullingen: Neske, 1959), p. 180. The adjective/adverb *jäh*, whose etymology is obscure, carries the sense of the precipitous, abrupt, sudden.
85. *Ibid.*, p. 182.
86. *Ibid.*, p. 181.
87. Cf. *Questions IV, op. cit.*, pp. 338–9. The 'Letter on Humanism', *op. cit.*, p. 265, is where Heidegger

addresses the *'vorläufiges Wesen des Denkens'* that must be understood as the conjunction of the preliminary character of thought; it does not rest upon itself since it is the gift of being in a verbal sense, with its pre-cursory character that comes from its 'capacity' to leap directly into being rather than remaining 'in the wake' of beings.

88. See, for example, Heidegger, 'Vom Wesen und Begriff der Physis' ("On the Essence and Concept of Physis") in *Wegmarken* (Frankfurt am Main: Klostermann, 1967), p. 311 ff.; French trans. in *Questions II* (Paris: Gallimard, 1968), p. 211 (see the translator's note).
89. *Questions IV, op. cit.*, p. 338.
90. *Ibid.*, p. 339.
91. *Wegmarken*, *op. cit.*, p. 319. See the long translator's note in *Questions II*, *op. cit.*, p. 193 ff.
92. *Ibid.*, p. 339: 'In conceiving there is in effect a grasping gesture. The Greek ορισμος, on the contrary, tenderly surrounds what the look takes into view; it does not conceive.'

3 Logic and Metaphysics

1. W. von Humboldt, *Über die Verschiedenheiten des menschlichen Sprachbaues und ihren Einfluss auf die geistige Entwicklung des Menschengeschlechts* (1830–5) in his collected works, (Berlin: Behr, 1907), vol. 7, 1, pp. 212–13 (henceforth UVS): *'Die wirkliche Gegenwart der Synthesis muss gleichsam immateriell in*

der Sprache sich offenbaren, man muss inne werden, dass sie, gleich einem Blitze, dieselbe durchleuchtet und die su verbinden Stoffe, wie eine Glut aus unbekannten Regionen, ineinander verschmolzen hat.' See Humboldt, *On Language: the diversity of human language structure and its influence on the mental development of mankind*, trans. Peter Heath (Cambridge: Cambridge University Press, 1988), p. 184.

2. See, in Heidegger, *Beiträge zur Philosophie* (Frankfurt am Main: Klostermann, 1989), §37, pp. 78–9, the paragraph entitled 'Das Seyn und seine Erschweigung (die Sigetik)' ("Being and its Reticence (the Sigetic)") of which there follows a provisional translation:

   > The fundamental question: *how does being occur* [*wie west das Seyn*]? Explicit reticence [*die Erschweigung*] is the considered legality of being silent [*Erschweigens*] (σιγαν). Explicit reticence is the 'logic' of philosophy, the fundamental question. It seeks the truth of *the event of the occurrence* of being [Wahrheit der Wesung *des Seyns*], and this truth is the signalling and ringing concealment [*die winkend-anklingende Verborgenheit*] (the secret) of *Ereignis* (the hesitant refusal) [*die zögernde Versagung*]. We cannot immediately say being itself at the very moment it springs forth in the leap, as every saying comes from being and speaks from its

> truth. All speech and thus all logic are under the domination of being. The essence of 'logic' (see the course from the summer semester of 1934) is consequently the 'sigetic'. It is only in the 'sigetic' that the essence of language can attain understanding. But 'sigetic' is a rubric only for those who still think in 'disciplines' [*Fächern*] and believe they possess knowledge only when what is said is classed amongst them.

Heidegger refers in a note to the end of the course from the summer semester of 1937 on Nietzsche where it is said that 'the highest saying that thinks consists not simply in being silent in the saying over what is properly to be said, but in saying it in such a way that it is named precisely in the non-saying. Saying as being silent [*Erschweigen*]' (GA 44, 1986, p. 233). It follows from these two texts that what is at issue is not being silent, but rather making silence come to pass in speech: this is the 'performative' sense of ***Er****schweigen*.

3. Allow me to refer here to my article 'Logic and Ontology: Heidegger's "Destruction" of Logic', *Research in Phenomenology*, vol. 17, 1987, pp. 55–74.
4. *Sein und Zeit* (Tübingen: Niemeyer, 1953), p. 25; English-language trans., *Being and Time*, trans. J. Stambaugh (Albany, NY: SUNY PRESS, 1996). Heidegger says here of Aristotle that he no longer understood dialectic because he located it through

a movement of *Aufhebung*, sublation, on a more radical ground: '*weil er sie auf einen radikaleren Boden stellte und **aufhob***' (my italics). The last word is rigorously untranslatable, since it can mean here, just as with Hegel, only the simultaneity of an abolition, of a conservation and of an elevation (*tollere, conservare, elevare*). See in this connection Heidegger, *Hegel's Phenomenology of Spirit*, the lecture course of the winter semester 1930–1, GA 32 (Bloomington: Indiana University Press, 1988), p. 28, as well as Heidegger, *Hebel, der Hausfreund* (Pfullingen: Neske, 1965), p. 11.

5. A term associated by Heidegger with 'inexplicit' to characterise the temporal orientation of the Greek understanding of being.
6. By hyphenating this word I am attempting to translate the German word *vorhanden*. See in this connection notes 2 and 7 (p. 122 and 124) in my book, *Heidegger et la question du temps* ("Heidegger and the Question of Time") (Paris: P.U.F., 1990).
7. Cf. *Sein und Zeit*, *op. cit.*, pp. 21–2.
8. *Ibid.*, p. 22.
9. *Ibid.*, p. 33.
10. *An Introduction to Metaphysics*, trans. Ralph Manheim (New Haven, CT and London: Yale University Press, 1959), p. 187.
11. One can use the Husserlian vocabulary here with its geological metaphor since it is still a question with Heidegger also – at least before the 'turn' – as it

already was with Hegel, of accounting for manifestations of death in which the 'living present', ungraspable in itself, is given to an always already historical 'natural attitude'. It is a matter of 'bearing what death is' (*das Tote festzuhalten*) and of remaining in it, of 'converting' it into being, as Hegel puts it in a famous passage of the Preface to the *Phenomenology of Spirit*. To tell the truth, philosophy has never had, from Platonic anamnesis to the Husserlian questioning back and to Heideggerian 'de-construction', any other project than this 'return upstream'. It is not without reason that Heidegger affirms at the end of the 'Letter on Humanism' that 'essential thinkers always say the same. But that does not mean: the identical.' But it is no less true that such a statement may seem arbitrary, at least to those who have not yet made thinking their 'only' task, since these thinkers 'only say it for one who attempts to think in their traces'.

12. *Sein und Zeit*, *op. cit.*, p. 22.
13. *Ibid.*, p. 161. In relation to the status of language in Heidegger's thought allow me to refer to my article 'Language and *Ereignis*' in *Reading Heidegger. Commemorations*, ed. John Sallis (Bloomington: Indiana University Press, 1992), pp. 357–69.
14. *Ibid.* '*Den Bedeutungen wachsen Worte zu. Nicht aber werden Wörterdinge mit Bedeutungen versehen*' ('Words accrue to meanings. But word-things are not provided subsequently with meanings'). We

can already discern here the distinction between *Worte* (words in the sense of what is said [*paroles*]) and *Wörter* ('terms'), a distinction subsequently of cardinal importance to Heidegger. See in this connection my article 'La pensée comme traduction: Autour de Heidegger' ("Thought as Translation: On Heidegger") forthcoming in the proceedings of the conference 'La traduction des philosophes' ("The Translation of Philosophers") (Publications de la Sorbonne).

15. We find here the Husserlian conception of language. See in relation to this J. Derrida, 'Form and Meaning: A Note on the Phenomenology of Language' in *Margins of Philosophy* (Chicago: University of Chicago Press, 1982), p. 155 ff. The anachronism consists in regarding utterances [*paroles*] as being born of pre-existing meanings whereas, as Humboldt has shown, it is language itself as such that is at the origin of meaning, which can be detached from its 'grammatical clothing' only through abstraction.
16. *Sein und Zeit*, *op. cit.*, p. 165.
17. *Ibid.*, §18.
18. *Ibid.*, p. 87. This signi-*ficare* does not consist only in the imposition of meanings on 'things'. It is above all a reflective self-signification of Dasein to itself, and it is this 'reflection', this return to self in the 'for the sake of which' (*Worumwillen*, which corresponds to Aristotle's ου ενεκα and the Kantian *Endzweck*) in the totality of referential

relations (*Bewandtnis*) of which the worldhood of the world is composed, that constitutes, as we shall see, the 'articulation' of the understanding in interpretation.

19. *Ibid*. The term '*fundieren*' [founding] clearly refers to the Husserlian problem of the grounding of the 'categorial' in the sensible. It is unsurprising then to find the following marginal note to this sentence in the '*Hüttenexemplar*' [see above, chapter 2, note 34]: '*Unwahr. Sprache ist nicht aufgestockt, sondern* ist *das ursprünglicher Wesen der Wahrheit als Da*.' ('False. Language is not supported, but is the originary essence of truth as There.')
20. *Ibid*., p. 165.
21. *Ibid*. 'Ontology of the pre-sent being' translates the expression '*Ontologie des Vorhandenen*'.
22. *Ibid*., p. 224.
23. Cf. Husserl, *Shorter Works,* ed. Peter McCormick and Frederick A. Elliston (Brighton: Harvester Press, 1981), p. 154. It was Husserl who defined Bolzano's 'propositions in themselves' as 'mythical entities suspended between being and non-being' and who emphasised that it was the 'profound assimilation' of Lotze's reflections on Plato's theory of forms that gave him 'the key to the curious conceptions of Bolzano's'. Allow me to refer in this connection to my article 'Husserl, Lotze et la logique de la "validité" ' ("Husserl, Lotze and the logic of 'validity"), *Kairos*, 5, 1994, pp. 31–48.

24. I have briefly discussed this special status of discourse in *Heidegger et la question de temps* (Paris: P.U.F., 1990), pp. 70 and 77–8.
25. *Sein und Zeit*, *op. cit.*, p. 161.
26. *Ibid.*, p. 147. We are still dealing with phenomenology here because the relation to sight and seeing continues structurally to define Dasein. This phenomenology is hermeneutic because this sight is itself founded on the 'circle' inherent to all projection inasmuch as it 'articulates' the being sighted in relation to the ontological horizon that gives it meaning.
27. *Ibid.* A marginal note in the *Hüttenexamplar* [see above, note 19] specifies that 'thought' must be understood here in the traditional sense of διανοια or *Verstand*, but that one must not understand *Verstehen* (the existential) on the basis of *Verstand* (the understanding). Heideggerian *Verstehen* does not simply mean *intelligere*, it must be understood on the basis of the etymology of the term *vor-stehen* (to which Heidegger makes a brief allusion in *Sein und Zeit*, p. 143) which allies it with the Greek επιστημη, as Heidegger recalls in the Le Thor seminar of 1969, *Questions IV* (Paris: Gallimard, 1976), *op. cit.*, p. 268: 'Understanding, *Verständnis*, must in turn be understood in the primary sense of *Vorstehen*: being stood up before, being on a level with, being at the measure of supporting that before which one is.'
28. *Sein und Zeit*, *op. cit.*, p. 148.

29. *Ibid*., p. 149.
30. *Ibid*., p. 150.
31. *Ibid*. This is a cardinal point which one cannot stress too much: the interpretation of 'something as something' (*Etwas als Etwas*) in no way transforms a pre-sent being into a ready-to-hand being, a pure 'sensible' given into a thing endowed with meaning, but consists solely in the originary repetition through which a being is *identified* on the basis of its difference with respect to the meaningfulness of the totality of the world, which is always already projected. As Heidegger explicitly emphasises in §32 (*op. cit.*, p. 150 ff.), the *Als-struktur* (the 'as' structure) of interpretation is founded on the *Vor-struktur* (the structure of anticipation) of understanding of which, nevertheless, it constitutes only the development. The articulation of these two structures is at the origin of meaning, and this articulation is as Heidegger will subsequently see, nothing other than the opening of the ontico-ontological difference itself.
32. *Ibid*., p. 151.
33. As Heidegger emphasises (*op. cit.*, p. 152), it arises from a 'ground' (*Grund*) that itself becomes accessible only in the clearing of meaning.
34. In the Husserlian notion of 'fulfilment', itself the corollary of the anticipation of meaning, we find evidence that this *circular* structure of meaning had been seen not only by Kant, but also by Husserl. Heidegger alludes to this with the sentence (*op. cit.*,

p. 151): 'Only Dasein "has" meaning in that the disclosedness of being-in-the-world can be "fulfilled" by the beings discoverable in it.'

35. *Ibid.*, p. 155. [tn Joan Stambaugh translates the sentence to which this passage refers as: ' "Positing the subject" dims beings down to focus on "the hammer there" in order to let what is manifest be seen *in* its determinable definite character through this dimming down.']
36. *Ibid.*, p. 158.
37. *Ibid.*, p. 159.
38. *Ibid.*, p. 160. A marginal note in the *Hüttenexemplar* [see above, note 19] specifies that it is Husserl who is intended here.
39. Heidegger, 'Letter on Humanism' in *Basic Writings*, 2nd rev. edn, ed. D. F. Krell (New York: HarperCollins, 1993).
40. *An Introduction to Metaphysics*, *op. cit.*, p. 121. On the previous page Heidegger specifies that because 'logic as such remains questionable' it is necessary 'to place "logic" in quotes'.
41. 'Letter on Humanism', *op. cit.*, p. 221. Heidegger uses the verb *ersetzen* here.
42. *Ibid.*, p. 219: '*Das Sein als Element des Denkens ist in der technischen Auslegung des Denkens preisgegeben*.' Roger Munier's French translation renders this as: 'Being as the element of thinking is abandoned in the technical interpretation of thinking.' The term *preisgegeben* that I prefer to translate here by 'sacrifice' rather than 'abandon' is a translation of

the French *'donner en prise'* and has the strong sense of *livrer en proie*, 'to betray, to prostitute'. However, as is natural to a German ear, Heidegger perhaps understands by this word less the French *'prise'* than the German *Preis*, ('price'), as is confirmed by the subsequent appearance of the terms *Markt,* ('market') (p. 219) and *Wettbewerbe,* ('competition') (p. 221) that say a good deal about Heidegger's 'mercantile' conception of the Sophists as a founding moment of this technical interpretation of thinking in relation to which philosophy is only a reaction. See in this connection *What is Philosophy?* (London: Vision Press, 1963), p. 51, where 'the attack of Sophist reasoning which always had ready for everything an answer which was comprehensible to everyone and which they put on the market' is once again at issue. That the Sophist sells his knowledge as goods signals the 'decline' of thinking reduced, in this way, to something possessing nothing more than an instrumental 'value', a state of affairs confirmed by the traditional definition of logic as οργανον or κανων. This explains why Heidegger can declare that in this way 'we judge thinking by an inappropriate measure' as 'this way of judging is equivalent to the procedure of trying to evaluate the essence and resources of a fish by seeing how long it can live on dry land' (*op. cit.*, p. 219).

43. *Ibid.*, p. 218.
44. Heidegger, *What is Called Thinking?*, trans. J.

Glenn Gray (New York: Harper and Row, 1968), p. 154. See also, *On the Way to Language*, trans. Peter D. Hertz (New York: Harper and Row, 1971), p. 8.

45. Cf. 'Letter on Humanism', *op. cit.*, p. 218.
46. *Ibid.*, p. 221.
47. Allow me to refer on this point to my article 'La fin de la philosophie et le commencement de la pensée' ("The end of philosophy and the beginning of thought") in *Heidegger: Questions ouvertes* ("Heidegger: Open Questions") (C.I.P., Osiris, 1988), in particular, pp. 125–7.
48. Cf. 'Letter on Humanism', *op. cit.*, p. 221 ff. where it is made clear that the very concept of the school is meaningful only in the context of a technical interpretation of thinking, every school being in the end a 'technical' school. Already in 1935, in *An Introduction to Metaphysics* (*op. cit.*, p. 121), Heidegger noted that the formation of logic began 'at the moment when Greek philosophy reached its end and became a school matter, of organisation and technique'.
49. See in this connection Paul Ricoeur, *The Rule of Metaphor*, trans. Robert Czerny with Kathleen McLaughlin and John Costello (London: Routledge, 1978), p. 311 who after deploring the 'spirit of vengefulness' that presides over 'the enclosure of the previous history of Western thought within the unity of "the" metaphysical' and rightly considering the latter to be an 'after-

the-fact construction', declares that: 'It seems to me time to deny oneself the convenience, which has become a laziness in thinking, of lumping the whole of Western thought together under a single word, metaphysics.' This is a criticism echoed by Jacques Derrida who, replying to Paul Ricoeur and refusing to allow his own problem to be taken as a 'radicalisation of the Heideggerian movement that is *continuous* with it', affirms that: 'It is not a question for me of taking "metaphysics" ['*la*' *metaphysique*] as the homogeneous unity of a totality. I have never believed in the existence of such a thing as *the* "metaphysical" [la *metaphysique*]': *Psyche* (Paris: Galilée, 1987), p. 72. A convenience, at once lazy and vengeful or an unwarranted process of homogenisation, in both cases the very *identity* of the West and of its history is put in question to the extent that it is rooted (as Husserl already said and saw in this nothing less than a 'revolution within historicity') in the appearance of the philosophical attitude of θεωρια, a way of characterising thinking that, for Heidegger, 'already occurs within the "technical" interpretation of thinking' as 'a reactive attempt to preserve the autonomy of thinking over against acting and doing' ('Letter on Humanism', *op. cit.*, p. 219). What cannot, it appears to me, be denied is less the 'identity' of the West itself than the fact that the West could, as a historical process, have consisted only in a *continuous promotion of the One and of Identity* (not only from the scientific,

but also from the religious and political, points of view), as the Westernisation of the planet which is also a 'uni-formisation' bears witness today. Doubtless, this history is more the result of a sum of chance occurrences than the development of a programme: it remains the case though that from the *retrospective* point of view of uni-fication (*un* ***regard uni-ficateur***], which remains Western and philosophical (Heidegger would simply say 'Greek'), it is possible precisely to safeguard the originality of 'great beginnings' other than the Greek and to initiate a dialogue with them that would be alienating neither for them nor for us, to identify, in the mode of the future anterior and under the *assumed name* of 'metaphysics', the long and *free* historical *sequence* whose provisional result we are, we who can speak only with others – and it is a condition common to all – under the protection and by means of names that are at once 'posthumous' and 'fore-runners' in the 'responsibility' of an 'after the event' that signals the finitude of all thinking.

50. 'Letter on Humanism', *op. cit.*, p. 220.
51. J. Beaufret, *Le poème de Parménid,* (Paris: P.U.F., 1955), p. 35.
52. In *The Principle of Reason* (Indiana: Indiana University Press, 1991), p. 124, after having emphasised that under the constraint of the demand for the rendering of sufficient reasons for all things, 'the fundamental character of contem-

porary human existence that everywhere works for certainty is consolidated', Heidegger remarks that 'Leibniz, the discoverer of the fundamental principle of sufficient reason, was also the inventor of "life insurance" '.

53. Cf. Heidegger, *Identität und Differenz* (Pfullingen: Neske, 1957); English-language edn, *Identity and Difference*, trans. Joan Stambaugh (New York: Harper and Row, 1969), p. 50. Heidegger emphasises in this passage that the retrocessive move of a 'step back' precisely does not have the result of a 'construction' after the event or an 'objectivisation' of the past, but consists, on the contrary, in letting the totality of the history of Western thought *come* to us in an 'over against' [*en-face*] (*Gegenüber*) that is not an objective (*Gegenstand*) representation. Heidegger refers here to a passage in *The Principle of Reason* (*op. cit.*, p. 87) where it is explicitly emphasised that in the *Gegenüber*, the *Gegen* (the against) reveals itself not through the objectivising 'throw' on the part of the 'subject' (*Gegenstand* says first of all in German, as Heidegger recalls, *Gegenwurf*, 'throw against', on the basis of a literal translation of the Latin *objectum*), but through what comes to humans (*über den Menschen kommt*) and surprises them (*was den Menschen überkommt*). Here coming after the event is the modality of a thinking that wants to be, not the foundation and seizure of the things of the past (*Das Vergangene*), but the reception and de-finition of a 'presence'

(*Anwesen*) of what has been and comes to us from the future.

54. *Ibid.*, p. 57.
55. *Ibid.* See *Identität und Differenz*, *op. cit.*, p. 54. The verb *prägen*, which bears the sense of imprinting, striking, forging, engraving, is probably derived from the Indo-European root **bhreg-* which gave *brechen* (to break) in German and *frangere* and *fragmentum* in Latin. One must understand by this term, as used here, the imposition of a form which is at the same time the possibility of a break-through, of a way out of withdrawal.
56. *Ibid.*, p. 66.
57. Cf. Heidegger, 'Einleitung zu Was ist Metaphysik?' ('Introduction to "What is Metaphysics?"') in *Wegmarken*, (Frankfurt am Main: Klostermann, 1967), p. 208.
58. *Identität und Differenz*, *op. cit.*, p. 55 : '*Daher ist alle Metaphysik im Grunde vom Grunde aus das Gründen, das vom Grunde die Rechenschaft gibt, ihm Rede steht und ihn schliesslich zur Rede stellt*' ('Therefore all metaphysics is at bottom, and from the ground up, what grounds, what gives account of the ground, what is called to account by the ground, and finally what calls the ground to account': trans. p. 58). The expressions '*jemandem Rede stehen*' and '*jemanden zur Rede stellen*' certainly mean respectively 'be called to account by someone' and 'call someone to account', but the term *Rede* must here be taken in the sense of discourse since, as Heidegger remarks

'in passing' (*'sei nur beilaüfig bemerkt', op. cit.*, p. 67, trans. p. 69) 'the same λογος also contains within itself the imprint (*Prägung*) of the being of language, and thus determines the way of utterance as a logical way in the broadest sense'.

59. Cf. *Identity and Difference*, *op. cit.*, pp. 70–1. The One doubles up as αρχη and as τελος, as generality and unity, explaining why being is the ground of beings but why a supreme being, in turn, grounds being in reason, even if, from the point of view of difference, being and beings gravitate about one another. This is the fundamental structure of metaphysics, and it became the *explicit* schema of experience and reflection in German Idealism. See in this connection my short book *Hölderlin. Tragédie et Modernité*, ("Hölderlin. Tragedy and Modernity") (Fougères: Encre Marine, 1992), pp. 51–2.
60. *Ibid.*, p. 58.
61. *Ibid.*, pp. 61–2.
62. *Ibid.*, p. 71.
63. *Ibid.*, pp. 62 and 65.
64. *Ibid.*, p. 65. In *Unterwegs zur Sprache* (Pfullingen: Neske, 1959), p. 24 ff.; English-language trans., see 'Language' in *Poetry, Language, Thought*, trans. Albert Hofstadter (New York: Harper and Row, 1971), p. 202 ff. Heidegger uses the Hölderlinian term *Innigkeit* (intimacy) to speak of the same *Unter-schied* (difference) and of the same split that yields the separation on the basis of which world

and thing, being and beings, arise. This separation which is *at the same time* a joining, is the separation of the same differing 'originarily' from itself and not the difference between two terms that could be subsequently unified. Heidegger's thought is a thought of the same and not of the one.

65. *Ibid.*, p. 65. The term *Austrag* certainly has the sense of 'settlement', 'arrangement', 'conciliation' and 'arbitration', which is why the French translator André Préau, following a suggestion of Heidegger's, translates it as 'conciliation' after having recalled in *Questions I* (Paris: Gallimard, 1968), p. 236, that it is the literal German translation of the Latin *dis-fero* (*tragen*, 'to draw', stems from a root that is found only in Germanic languages). But the verb *austragen* also means to distribute, to hawk, to carry to the end and to carry to term. In *Unterwegs Zur Sprache* (*op. cit.*, p. 22; English-language trans., 'Language', *op. cit.*, p. 200) Heidegger connects this verb with the Old German *bern*, *bären*, 'to bear', found today in *gebären,* (to give birth) and *Gebärde* (gesture).
66. *Ibid.*, p. 67.
67. 'Letter on Humanism', *op. cit.*, p. 218.
68. *Identity and Difference*, *op. cit.*, p. 73 ff.
69. I am borrowing here, in a somewhat illicit fashion, this written form from Jacques Derrida, to designate the *event* of difference that makes of difference something wholly other than an added-on

distinction. Heidegger, employing the resources belonging to the German language, designates this with the term *Unter-schied*, a term that is untranslatable in French.

70. I shall mention only a single example here, admittedly a paradigmatic one, of this 'translation': while Husserl often prefers to use the foreign term ειδος rather than the German term *Wesen*, tainted with ambiguity (cf. *Ideas*, trans. W. R. Boyce Gibson (London: Allen and Unwin, 1931), p. 56), Heidegger positions himself, on the contrary, at the very heart of this polysemy of the German term to play on the contrast between the traditional meaning (resulting from an historical sedimentation) of *Wesen* as a term used to translate the Latin *essentia* and the properly historial meaning, which can still be heard in ordinary words such as *anwesend* (present) and *abwesend* (absent), that relates to being understood as duration and deployment (*das Währende*) and not to being understood as quiddity. See in this connection *On the Way to Language*, *op. cit.*, p. 94 ff.
71. One might consider the contribution of *Sein und Zeit*/*Being and Time* to this necessary metamorphosis to be essentially lexical – see for example the terms *Geworfenheit, Befindlichkeit, Zeitigung*, etc.; a list of the words made up by Heidegger is to be found in Erasmus Schöfer's *Die Sprache Heideggers* ("Heidegger's Language") (Pfullingen: Neske, 1962), p. 67 ff. Nevertheless, one must bear

in mind that at this time Heidegger already emphasises that for the task of 'repeating' the question of being, 'we lack not only most of the words but, above all, the "grammar"' (*Sein und Zeit, op. cit.*, p. 39).

72. *On the Way to Language*, *op. cit.*, p. 136.
73. *Ibid.*, p. 35.
74. Humboldt, *UVS*, vol. 7, 1, §12, p. 46. Quoted by Heidegger in *Unterwegs zur Sprache*, *op. cit.*, p. 247; see *On the Way to Language*, *op. cit.*, p. 116–17.
75. *Ibid.*, p. 93. Significantly, *Unterwegs zur Sprache* ends with this quotation.
76. In the Vedic tradition and, in particular, in Patanjali (who is thought to have lived between the 2nd century BC and the 5th century AD and who continued the work of Panini) one finds the idea that the essence of speech is neither the material sound nor the spirit but the indissociable unity of the two, an idea that he expresses with the term *sfota* meaning at once what is manifested and what manifests. This term, besides its 'philosophical' sense, rightly means 'explosion', from the radical *sphut*: to explode, to crack, to tear, to open oneself. The divine character of speech is thus there also understood on the basis of the opening of difference. What characterises Vedic thought is the fact that it approached its own concept of the absolute (*brahman*) via the intermediary of the power ascribed to speech as the principal instrument of sacrificial rite.

77. *Ibid.*, p. 329. Quoted by Heidegger in *Unterwegs zur Sprache*, *op. cit.*, p. 248; *On the Way to Language*, *op. cit.*, p. 118.
78. Cf. *Unterwegs zur Sprache*, *op. cit.*, p. 268; *On the Way to Language*, *op. cit.*, p. 136.
79. *UVS*, p. 16–17.
80. Humboldt employs the term *Emanation* here, from the Latin verb *emanare*, to flow out.
81. Cf. *Unterwegs zur Sprache*, *op. cit.*, pp. 203 and 244; *On the Way to Language*, *op. cit.*, pp. 96 and 114. The French translator François Fédier consequently translated *Sprache* as 'parole' throughout, whilst I have opted to retain the traditional translation of 'langage' or 'langue' to avoid any ambiguity, given the French habit of opposing, in a Saussurian vein, the ideal 'system' of a language to 'discourse' [*parole*] understood as the activity of a speaking subject. This distinction has no strict equivalent in German. In particular, one must be careful not to confuse it with the *Sprache / Rede* opposition which originated with Humboldt, solely because Humboldt would never have accepted Saussure's thesis according to which 'the vocal organs are just as external to language as the electrical apparatus that serve to transcribe Morse code are to that code': (*Course in General Linguistics*, trans. Wade Baskin (London: Peter Davies, 1960), p. 18 , since this thesis, including the accompanying comparison of language to a symphony, a 'reality' independent of its execution,

amounts to thinking of language as a semiotic practice deliberately set to work by peoples, a view which is a product of the 'anachronism' of describing history with the aid of its end products (the notion of the sign and spoken word). Humboldt is particularly clear on this point: 'It is impossible to conceive of the genesis of language (*Sprache*) as a process that would begin with the designation of object with words (*Wörter*) and then assemble them together. In reality, discourse (*Rede*) is not composed of pre-existent words, on the contrary it is discourse as a whole that gives rise to words' (*UVS*, p. 72). If *Sprache* must be understood as the always singular unity of an intrinsically historical 'language' [*langue*] and 'discourse' [*parole*], then *Rede* constitutes its actuality that can be retained in works of literature and philosophy.

82. *UVS*, p. 53: 'The mutual accord of thought and sound, moreover, is very striking. As thought, comparable to a flash of lightning or a thunder clap, gathers the full force of representation in a single point and excludes concomitant material, in the same way sound rings out by detaching itself with a strongly marked unity.'
83. *UVS*, p. 66.
84. Cf. Ole Hansen-Love, *La revolution copernicienne du langage dans l'oeuvre de Wilhelm von Humboldt* ("The Copernican Revolution in Language in the Work of Wilhelm von Humboldt") (Paris: Vrin, 1972), p. 58 ff., citing in this connection Cassirer

who remarks in the *Philosophy of Symbolic Forms* that the concept of Organicism is not taken in Romanticism as the expression of a certain class of phenomena but as that of a universal speculative principle. As Pierre Caussat remarks elsewhere, the definition given by Humboldt of language as 'the totalising projection of speech in action' (*UVS*, p. 46) 'removes the hypothesis that lends weight to the concept of "organism"' since such a definition of language, even though it is organically conditioned as Humboldt himself says, makes it appear in 'the freedom of an indefinite transition' which raises it 'above Organicism' since 'nothing in it is static, everything dynamic' implying that 'one can only compare it with physiology and not with anatomy'; (see Humboldt, *On Language the diversity of human language structure and its influence on the moral development of mankind*, trans. Peter Heath (Cambridge: Cambridge University Press, 1988), p. 90.

85. *UVS*, p. 53.
86. *UVS*, p. 55. As J. Derrida emphasises in *Speech and Phenomena*, trans. David B. Allison (Evanston, IL: Northwestern University Press, 1973), p. 77: 'When I speak, it belongs to the phenomenological essence of this operation that *I hear myself at the same time* that I speak.' This circularity of the phonic exteriorisation of spirit returning in its own hearing in the form of its own product (*Erzeugniss*) constitutes the very structure of an

ipseity defined as the 'ability-to-hear-oneself speak'.

87. *UVS*, p. 69.
88. Cf. *Über die Verschiedenheiten des Menschlichen Sprachtbaues*, in his collected works, *op. cit.*, vol. 6, 1, §36, p. 152: 'But what thought, strictly speaking, needs to form concepts in language, is not properly what is effectively perceived by the ear; or, in other terms, if one distinguishes in the articulated sound the articulation and the divulging in sound (*Geräusch*), thought has need of the former but not of the latter.'
89. *UVS*, p. 66. In this passage, Humboldt, analysing the language acquisition of the deaf and dumb by looking at the movement of the organs of speech of others, emphasises that they also possess a 'faculty of articulation' and that they thus arrive at true language learning and not merely at the capacity to associate representations with signs or images. He considers the detour 'against nature' they must in this way make via vision in place of hearing (because they are deaf) to be the proof of the 'tight and profound' tie that writing maintains with language, even in the absence of the mediation of hearing. Far from opposing writing to speech, Humboldt considers both to be the transitory 'objectivisations' of spirit. The living temporality of language finds 'nowhere, not even in writing, a stable resting place', 'its, so to speak, dead part' before 'always being newly produced in thinking,

being newly brought back to life in discourse or understanding' (*op. cit.*, p. 63).

90. *UVS*, p. 65.
91. *UVS*, p. 63. We find here a sobriety comparable to Kant's in this decision to hold fast to the phenomena without attempting to give an explanation, which could only be 'mythic', of articulation, like the schematism, that 'art hidden in the depths of the human soul'. Now, this 'human nature' mentioned by Humboldt refers for him, before all else, to the upright posture 'denied to animals', to the extent that it is 'compatible' with linguistic sound, since 'discourse can only be deafened and expire by staying on the ground, it needs to be accompanied by the expression of the look and of the face, as well as hand gestures, and in this way to be surrounded by all that characterises humanity in the human being' (*op. cit.*, p. 55). This connection between language and an upright posture traditionally defines what is proper to the human. Humboldt, whilst staying within the limits and framework of his 'age', gives us a 'phenomenological' (and not a theological) understanding that accords uncannily with what science tells us today. The progress of paleontology (I am summarising here the view put forward by Jean-Louis Heim, Professor of Paleontology at the Museum of Mankind, Paris; see *Libération*, 24 June 1992), teaches us that human language depends on many additional factors: a biostatic factor, the flexibility of the base

of the skull permitting the low position of the larynx allowing the latter to be ventilated by the lungs, which gives language its guttural character (and not simply lingual as with parrots); a cerebral and neurological factor, the flexibility of the base of the skull being accompanied by a tipping of the occipital and a moving forward of the frontal allowing the skull to give greater space to the areas of the cortex situated between the frontal lobe and the occipital, in particular to the Wernicke centre which is the principal language centre; and finally a socio-cultural factor, the factor of a tradition that in itself demands communication. The flexibility of the base of the skull which follows directly from being a biped (when the human stands up, the head leans forward) immediately accompanies cerebral development. In this way, one can consider articulated language to be an epiphenomenon of being a biped.

92. *UVS*, pp. 54–5.
93. *UVS*, p. 95.
94. *UVS*, p. 213.
95. *Ibid.*, (my italics). See the interpretation of this passage in J. Lohmann, *Philosophie und Sprachwissenschaft* ("Philosophy and Linguistics") (Berlin: Dunker und Humblot, 1965), p. 191 ff.
96. Cf. *Unterwegs zur Sprache*, *op. cit.*, p. 249; *On the Way to Language*, *op. cit.*, p. 119. The reading of Humboldt offered by Heidegger here remains too schematic and is wanting in the generosity formerly

shown to Kant's thought. No more than it is possible to affirm categorically that Humboldt understands *energeia* 'in a manner wholly foreign to the Greek, in the sense of Leibniz's Monadology, as the activity of the subject', one cannot, in view of the texts cited here, maintain that he recognised in language only *one* of the forms of the vision of the world developed by human subjectivity. Instead, one ought to say that the idea of an original spontaneity, the idea of temporality itself, that Humboldt sees at work everywhere in human speech, explodes *from the interior* the epochal framework in which he continues to place himself, the framework of absolute subjectivity positing itself as being. The passage where Humboldt extends the genetic definition of the singular speech act (*das jedesmalige Sprechen*) to language (*Sprache*) as a whole bears witness to this, the latter being only 'the totality of what is said' (*UVS*, p. 46), which implies that it is *Sprache* in its creative 'intersubjectivity' which constitutes the very semantico-poetic process of history.

97. *UVS*, pp. 45–6. Here, already, finitude, the 'eternal' repetition of the 'synthetic' work of spirit, can be understood as the 'capacity' to give oneself a world.
98. *UVS*, p. 212.
99. *UVS*, p. 214.

4 THE LOGOS OF MORTALS

1. *Unterwegs zur Sprache* (Pfullingen: Neske, 1959) p. 215; *On the Way to Language*, trans. Peter D. Hertz (New York: Harper and Row, 1971), p. 107: '*Das Wesensverhältnis zwishen Tod und Sprache blizt auf, ist aber noch ungedacht.*'
2. Cf. *UVS*, p. 46. The spatialising moment of writing that provides only an 'incomplete and mummified conservation' of *Sprache* [speech], does not on its own take into account the objectivisation that already comes about with the 'temporal' materiality of articulated sound.
3. Preface to *The Phenomenology of Spirit*, trans. J. N. Findlay (Oxford: Oxford University Press, 1977), p. 19 (my italics).
4. *Ibid.*
5. *Ibid.*, p. 37.
6. *Ibid.* '*Der feste Boden, den das Räsonieren an dem ruhenden Subjekte hat, schwankt also, und nur diese Bewegung selbst wird der Gegenstand*' ('The solid ground which argument has in the passive subject is therefore shaken, and only this movement itself becomes the object'). The verb Hegel uses here is not *beugen*, a term used by Humboldt alongside *Flektion*, but *schwanken*, whose ordinary meaning is 'to waver', 'to vacillate', but which, however, also refers to the adjective, little used today, *schwank*, meaning 'flexible'.
7. *Ibid.* It is clear that Hegel is here placing himself

in opposition to Aristotle's 'logical' solution to the problem of the Platonic χωρισμος (separation) since it consists precisely in viewing universals as simple attributes: 'We call substance (ουσια) what is not a predicate of a subject (το μη καθ' υποκειμενον). Now, a universal (το καθολον) is always the predicate of a subject (το μη καθ' υποκειμενον)' (*Metaphysics*, Z, 13, 1038 b 15).

8. *Ibid.*, p. 38.
9. *Ibid.*, p. 40.
10. *Ibid.*, p. 27: 'Time . . . is the existent [*étant-là*] concept itself' (*das daseiende Begriff*).
11. *Ibid.*, p. 40.
12. *Ibid.*, pp. 39–40. The attainment of 'philosophical proof' is what is at issue here, combining analytic and dialectic and constituting the very essence of dialectical logic.
13. *Ibid.*, p. 40.
14. *Ibid.*, p. 36.
15. *Ibid.*, pp. 35–6. The terms *Enthaltsamkeit* (abstention) and *Anstrengung des Begriffs* (effort, contention of the concept) call to mind here the Husserlian style of philosophy understood as *strenge Wissenschaft* (rigorous science). However, it is not merely science as a form of thought that is 'rigorous' here but the concept itself which is capable of contention inasmuch as it is 'pure self-movement' that one might almost call 'soul' since it con-tains all the figures of its exteriority.
16. *Ibid.*, p. 38: '*Der Rythmus resultiert aus der*

schwebenden Mitte und Vereiningung beider.' This comparison makes sense only when considered with regard to the German language which, as we know, is characterised by the opposition of the descending rhythm of the word and the ascending rhythm of the sentence. The accentuation of the radical, most often at the beginning of the word, that makes German a 'naturally' etymological language, imposes on the word a descending, deductive rhythm when atonal suffixes are added to the radical. This rhythm is counterbalanced by the synthetic character of the sentence that rises in the middle giving it an ascendant, inductive rhythm very different from the descendant and analytic rhythm of French or English. In truth, it is surprising that there has not been more thought given to the importance of the influence not only of the history of language but also of the formal structure of the sentence on the development of thinking. In this regard it should be possible to learn a great deal about the different conceptions of time that ensue from the opposition between the open 'progressive sequence', of which the French sentence consists, which progresses according to the sequential order of lived time and places the noun designating the substrate before its determinations, and the closed 'anticipatory sequence' employed by the German sentence which ends with the noun designating the substrate already described according to its determinations.

17. Cf. 'Grundsätze des Denken' ("The Basic Principles of Thought") in *Jahrbuch für Psychologie und Psychotherapie*, vol. 1/3, 1958.
18. We must briefly recall here that the term *speculatio*, which literally means spying and comes from *specto*, I look [from *spectare*, to examine], has borne the philosophical sense of contemplation since it was used by Boethius to translate the Greek θεορια. But this sense was forgotten by Saint Augustine and, above all, by Saint Thomas Aquinas who both derived *speculatio* from *speculum* (mirror) and related it to the word used by Saint Paul in his first Letter to the Corinthians, XIII, 12: 'For now we see through a glass, darkly; but then face to face: now I know in part; but then shall I know even as also I am known.' Knowledge through faith is, in effect, indirect and confused like vision via a metal mirror. This is the sense which the mystics retained, and it is from them that the German term *Spiegulation* comes (from *Spiegel*, mirror). This understanding of *speculatio* as *visio Dei*, to be found in Nicholas of Cusa, was transmitted to Hegel by Jacob Böhme and Swabian pietism (Bengel and Oetinger). This explains the pejorative sense that Kant gives to the word which he regards as defining the mode of thinking of Scholastic metaphysics. Hegel, on the contrary, completely reverses the sense of the word by referring it back to its 'theoretical' origin but without cutting it off from its mystical meaning, which leads him to see in speculation the identity

of the concept and of intuition. It is in this sense that he affirms in the *Differenzschrift*: '*Das transcendantale Wissen vereinigt beides, Reflexion und Anschauung; es ist Begriff und Sein zugleich*' 'Transcendental knowledge unites the two terms, reflection and intuition; it is at once concept and being'): see *Hegel Werke, Jenaer Schriften 1801–1807* (Frankfurt am Main: Suhrkamp, 1970), vol. 2, p. 126: It is on the basis of this speculative unity of transcendental knowledge that the task of philosophy is defined for Hegel as the task of bringing being and concept to the consciousness of their identity, which he calls, in a Schellingian manner, the 'construction' of the absolute in consciousness (*op. cit.*, p. 19). See in this connection W. C. Zimmerli, *Die Frage nach der Philosophie, Interpretationen zu Hegels 'Differenzschrift'* (Bonn: Bouvier, 1974), p. 99 ff.

19. Hegel, *Science of Logic*, trans. J. N. Findlay (London: Allen and Unwin, 1969), vol. 1, Introduction, p. 56.
20. 'Grundsätze des Denkens', *op. cit.*, p. 36.
21. Preface to the *Phenomenology of Spirit*, *op. cit.*, p. 19 (my italics).
22. Cf. 'Grundsätze des Denkens', *op. cit.*, p. 34.
23. *What is Called Thinking?*, trans. J. Glenn Gray (New York: Harper and Row, 1968), p. 238.
24. Cf. 'Urteil und Sein', in *Hölderlin Werke und Briefe* (Frankfurt am Main: Insel, 1969), vol. 2, p. 283; English-language trans. *Friedrich Hölderlin: essays*

and letters on theory, ed. and trans. Thomas Pfau (Albany, NY: SUNY Press, 1988), p. 37 (henceforth, *Essays*). One also finds the expression '*das Sein, im einzigen Sinn des Wortes*' ('being, in the single sense of the term') in the Preface to the penultimate version of *Hyperion*, written at the end of 1795. Cf. *Hölderlin Werke und Briefe*, vol. 1, p. 167.

25. See above all the essay of 1796 entitled 'On Religion', *Essays*, pp. 90–5. Allow me to refer here to my article 'Hölderlin. De la religion' ("Hölderlin. On religion") in the *Cahiers de Fontenay* and, with regard to the entire subsequent development, to work in progress on 'Hölderlin and philosophy' that will be presented as an attempt to articulate all of Hölderlin's theoretical essays.
26. 'Das Werden im Vergehen', *Essays*, pp. 96–100. This title, which is not Hölderlin's own, nevertheless faithfully describes the essay's content. Certainly, one finds, as Beissner indicates in his commentary on this essay in the *Grundlage der gesamten Wissenschaftlehre* of 1794 (Hamburg: Meiner, 1956), p. 179, that Hölderlin had read at the time of its publication the following sentence: '*Die charakteristiche Form des Wechsels in der Wirksamkeit ist* ein Entstehen durch ein Vergehen *(ein Werden durch ein Verschwinden)*' ('The characteristic form of change in the actual is *birth through perishing* (becoming through disappearance)'. Doubtless,

Hölderlin remembered the very terms employed here by Fichte but to continue reading Fichte's text suffices to see that the thought deployed there remains tied to an ontology of substance since it takes care to specify precisely that to think becoming one must 'abstract entirely from substance' as the latter 'does not enter into change'.

27. Cf. the last lines of the *Phenomenology of Spirit*, *op. cit.*: '*Beide zusammen [Geschichte und Wissenschaft], die begriffne Geschichte, bilden die Erinnerung und die Schädelstätte des absoluten Geistes, die Wirklichkeit, Wahrheit und Gewissheit seines Throns, ohne den er das leblose Einsame wäre*' ('The two together [History and Science], comprehended History, form alike the inwardizing and the Calvary of absolute Spirit, the actuality, truth, and certainty of his throne, without which he would be lifeless and alone'; trans. A. V. Miller (Oxford: Oxford University Press, 1977), p. 493). In his translation of 1991 Jean-Pierre Lefebvre translates *Schädelstatte* with 'Golgotha' to revive the etymological sense of the word 'Calvary' whose sense has been weakened in French by its use to denote 'stone crosses at crossroads' whilst in German the reference to the 'charnel-house', or to 'the hill and the sepulchre of Christ's Passion', remains clear.

28. Cf. 'Das Werden im Vergehen' §5, *Hölderlin Werke*, *op. cit.*, vol. 2, p. 641 ff.; see *Essays*, p. 98. The term *Herstellung* has here both the sense of 'production' and that of 'restitution'. The famous

passage from the Preface to the *Phenomenology of Spirit*, where the true is defined as a Bacchic revel, attests to the fact that Hegel had also thought the primacy of 'death' [disparaître]. In it, Hegel explicitly emphasises that 'the evanescent itself must, on the contrary, be regarded as essential, not as something fixed, cut off from the true, and left lying who knows where outside of it, any more than the true is to be regarded as something on the other side, positive and dead' (*op. cit.*, p. 27). But, as has already been and will again be emphasised, Hegel understands 'this movement of being born and dying' as the 'life' of the concept and not as the tragic life of that 'monster' in which the human being, as structurally open to the divine, consists.

29. Cf. §9 of the essay: 'the dissolution of the ideal-individual appears not as weakening and death but as a reviving, as growth, and the dissolution of the infinite-new not as destructive violence but as love and both together as a creative act (transcendental) whose essence consists in uniting the ideal-individual and the real-infinite': *Essays*, p. 99.
30. See §1 of the essay where it is said that only the coincidence in the 'genetic movement' of decline and beginning is 'like language, expression, sign, presentation of a living yet particular whole': *Essays*, p. 96.
31. The final version of the poem says precisely: '*Viel hat Morgen an,/Seit ein Gespräch wir sind und hören*

voneinander, / Erfahren der Mensch; bald sind wir aber Gesang' ('Much, from the morning onwards, / Since we have been a dialogue and have heard from one another, / Has human kind learnt; but soon we shall be song'; *Friedrich Hölderlin. Poems and fragments*, trans. Michael Hamburger (Cambridge: Cambridge University Press, 1980), p. 439).

32. Cf. Nietzsche, *Also sprach Zarathustra*, III (Das Ja-und-Amen-Lied): '*So aber spricht Vogel-Weisheit: "Siehe, es gibt kein Oben, kein Unten! Wirf dich umher, hinaus, zurück, du Leichter! singe! sprich nich mehr! – sind alle Worte nicht für die Schweren gemacht? Lügen dem Leichten nicht alle Worte? Singe! sprich nicht mehr!*" ' ('Behold, there is no above, no below! Fling yourself about, out, back, weightless bird! Sing! Speak no more! – are not all words made for the heavy? Do not all words lie to the light? Sing! Speak no more!'; from *Thus Spoke Zarathustra*, trans. R. J. Hollingdale (Harmondsworth: Penguin, 1961)).
33. *Essays*, p. 109.
34. *Ibid.*, p. 101.
35. *Ibid.*, p. 109.
36. Preface to the *Phenomenology of Spirit*, *op. cit.*, p. 32 ff.
37. *Essays*, p. 102.
38. Cf. 'Wie wenn am Feiertage': '*So fiel, wie Dichter sagen, da sie sichtbar / Den Gott zu sehen begehrte, sein Blitz auf Semeles Haus / Und Asche tödtlich*

getroffne gebar / Die Frucht des Gewitters, den heiligen Bacchus' ('So once, the poets tell, when she desired to see / The god in person, visible, did his lightning fall on Semele's house / And, ash mortally struck, she bore / The fruit of the storm, the holy Bacchus'). [*tn* The author cites Michel Deguy and François Fédier's translation from *Approches de Hölderlin*, (Paris: Gallimard, 1973), p. 66, but see also Michael Hamburger's translation of a different version of the poem, in *Friedrich Hölderlin. Poems and fragments*, *op. cit.*, p. 375.]

39. *Essays*, p. 107. Hölderlin himself mentions here the '*immer widerstreitende Dialog*' [ever-contending dialogue] of Sophocles's *Oedipus* and the *Ineinandergreifen* (mutual involvement) of the different parts of the dialogue but also mentions that of the dialogue and the chorus, the whole finishing 'brutally' (*factisch*) and not in a harmonious reconciliation since '*Alles ist Rede gegen Rede, die sich gegenseitig aufhebt*' (all is discourse against discourse, each abolishing the other). Such a dialogue aims, in effect, 'to tear apart the soul', with its 'irritated receptivity', of those who are listening to it since it is 'the language of a world' 'where God and man', despite the 'lacuna' that separates them, 'communicate in the all-forgetting form of infidelity'. This 'tearing' speech, which can be received only in the anger that gives birth to a counter-discourse, is the discordant polyphony of modernity where, however, there

endures the sharing of a ***Ge****-spräch* which tests itself in its very impossibility.

40. Heraclitus, fragment 54: ‘Αρμονιη αφανης φανερης κρεισσων’ which Heidegger translates as ‘*Fuge, die ihr Erscheinen versagt, ist hörenen Waltens als eine, die zum Vorschein kommt*’ (Jointure that refuses to manifest itself is of a higher order than that which appears); see ‘Hölderlins Erde und Himmel’ (‘Hölderlin’s Earth and Heaven’) in *Erlauterungen zu Hölderlins Dichtung* (“Elucidations of Hölderlin’s Poetry”), 5th edn. (Frankfurt am Main: Klostermann, 1981), p. 179.
41. *Ibid.*, p. 155, where Heidegger quotes the version of the hymn entitled ‘Grieschenland’ (‘Greece’) that contains the following lines after those that speak of the existence of God (*Daseyn Gottes*) as a storm (*Gewitter*): ‘*Und Rufe, wie hinausschauen, zur / Unsterblickkeit und Helden*’ (And calls, like looking out, for / Immortality and heroes’). The man who ‘questions’ heaven in this way (*ibid.*, p. 169) is, *par excellence*, the Greek, that is to say he who understands himself on the basis of the look towards the divine that allows him his standing upright, who defines himself as επι–σταμενος (‘skilled’ or ‘knowing’ because of his proximity to things) and who sees in ‘science’ (επιστημη), itself also named in this same poem (*ibid.*, p. 167), the foundation of human existence.
42. The secret named by Paul Celan in ‘Der Meridian’ (‘The Meridian’), *Ausgewählte Gedichte*

(Frankfurt am Main: Suhrkamp, 1968), p. 144 – in the lines I quote here, adding my own scansion to his – through combining the solitude of *Gedicht* with that to which it bears witness, by *standing* there: '*Das Gedicht ist* einsam. *Es ist einsam und* unterwegs. *Wer es schreibt bleibt ihm* mit*gegeben.* / *Aber* steht *das Gedicht nicht gerade dadurch, also schon* hier, in *der Begegnung* – im Geheimnis der Begegnung?' (The poem is *solitary*. It is solitary and *underway*. Who writes it remains going along *with* it. / But does the poem not precisely *stand* through this, therefore already *here*, *in* the encounter – *in the secret of the encounter*?). In the original, only the last four words are underlined. Doubtless, it has never been more impossible to translate the German *Gedicht* by the Greek ποιεσις, itself a late term designating the art of the Muses, the μουσικη τεχνη. Such a *Dichtung* (the word undeniably comes from the Latin *dictare*, 'to compose', but one can also relate it to *dichten*, a word of Germanic origin meaning 'to condense') manifests the most extreme con-densation of saying, itself born of a standing-with [con-tention] of thought to whose height the *Anstrengung des Begriffs* of which Hegel speaks does not, perhaps, attain.

43. Cf. Heidegger, 'Sprache und Heimat' ("Language and Home") (1960) in *Denkerfahrungen* ("The Experience of Thinking") (Frankfurt am Main: Klosterman, 1983), p. 88.

44. *Ibid.*, p. 112 (my italics). An earlier text devoted to 'Hebel, the Friend of the House' was published in 1958.
45. *Unterwegs zur Sprache*, *op. cit.*, p. 208; *On the Way to Language*, *op. cit.*, p. 101. The German *Stimme*, whose primary sense is 'agreement' (consider also the verb *stimmen*, 'to agree'), expresses in a wholly different way from the Latin *vox* (the sound emitted by the voice) this agreement in which the voice consists.
46. *Ibid.*, p. 213 ff/106 ff.

EPILOGUE

1. Fragment 64: 'τα δε παντα οιακιξει κεραυνος'.
2. Cf. Hegel, Preface to the *Phenomenology of Spirit*, trans. J. N. Findlay (Oxford: Oxford University Press, 1977), p. 10: 'The true is the process of its own becoming, the circle that presupposes its end as its goal, having its end also as its beginning; and only by being worked out to its end, is it actual.'
3. Cf. T. S. Eliot, 'Little Gidding' in the *Four Quartets* (London: Faber and Faber, 1989), p. 47: 'What we call the beginning is often the end / And to make an end is to make a beginning. / The end is where we start from.'
4. Heidegger, *Unterwegs zur Sprache* (Pfullingen: Neske, 1959) p. 213; English-language edn, *On the Way to Language*, trans. Peter D. Hertz (New York: Harper and Row, 1971) p. 106: '*die Gegen-wart, die*

uns entgegenwartet und sonst die Zukunft heisst.' Heidegger is playing here on the word *Gegenwart*, the German word for the present but which literally means what, turned towards us, waits for us and is therefore the future in its literal meaning.

5. Merleau-Ponty, *Le visible et l'invisible* (Paris: Gallimard, 1964), p. 252; English-language edn, *The Visible and the Invisible*, trans. Alphonso Lingis (Evanston, IL: Northwestern University Press, 1968), p. 199.
6. It is in *Περι* Ψυχης that Aristotle affirms, as Heidegger emphasises in *Sein und Zeit* (Tübingen: Niemeyer, 1953), p. 14; English-language edn, *Being and Time*, trans. J. Stambaugh (Albany, NY: SUNY Press, 1996); that 'the soul is in a way all beings' (Aristotle, *De Anima*, 431 b 21) because in it there is an intellect 'capable of becoming all things' (*Ibid.*, 430 b 14).
7. Heidegger was already speaking in *The Essence of Reasons*, trans. Terrence Malick (Evanston, IL: Northwestern University Press, 1969), p. 99, note 59, of the 'ec-static, or *ek-centric* essence of Dasein'.
8. This is the case, *par excellence*, with Hölderlin – allow me to refer here to my book, *Hölderlin. Tragédie et modernité* ("Hölderlin. Tragedy and Modernity") (Fougères: Encre Marine, 1992) p. 79 ff.) but also with T. S. Eliot for whom the gathering of time in the point of the present constitutes the most constant theme of the *Four*

Quartets, *op. cit*.

9. Heidegger, in affirming that 'Time itself in the entirety of its deployment does not move and is immobile and at peace' (*On the Way to Language*, p. 106), echoes Kant and Husserl who both saw in the interior of temporal flow itself the presence of a time that remains and does not change. (Allow me to refer in this connection to my article 'Le temps et l'autre chez Husserl et Heidegger' ("Time and the Other in Husserl and Heidegger") in *Alter, Revue de Phénoménologie*, 1, 1993, p. 399 ff).
10. Cf. Heidegger. *Identity and Difference*, trans. Joan Stambaugh (New York: Harper and Row, 1969), in particular p. 40, and 'The Turning' in *The Question Concerning Technology and Other Writings* (New York: Harper, 1977), p. 41 ff.
11. T. S. Eliot, 'Burnt Norton' in *Four Quartets*, *op. cit.*, p. 15.
12. See what Heidegger says of Western languages at the end of *Identity and Difference*, *op. cit.*, p. 73 ff., a passage that echoes §20 of *Beyond Good and Evil*, trans. Walter Kaufmann (New York: Vintage Books, 1966), p. 27, in which Nietzsche (close here to Humboldt) recognised the unitary grammatical foundation of the 'strange family resemblance of all Indian, Greek and German philosophising' and raised the question of the doubtless wholly different interpretations of the world that thinkers belonging to other language groups would develop.

13. Cf. J. Derrida, *The Post Card*, trans. Alan Bass (Chicago: University of Chicago Press, 1987), pp. 128, 189, 197. With a certain distance from such a conception that sees in writing a *via negativa*, Nietzsche says this in §93 of *The Gay Science*: 'I am annoyed and ashamed of my writing; writing is for me a pressing and embarrassing need . . . I have not discovered any other way of *getting rid* of my thoughts', trans. Walter Kaufmann (New York: Random House, 1974), p. 146.
14. Cf. the French translator's note to *Acheminement vers la parole* (Paris: Gallimard, 1976), p. 109; English-language edn, *On the Way to Language*, *op. cit*. While *Zeichen* (sign in the sense of a mark or index) indirectly designates a thing not actually present, the *Wink* (sign in the sense of gesture) makes something immediately evident, makes what is to be thought appear directly. It is in this sense that Heidegger lets it be understood that making a sign is the fundamental trait of language.
15. Heidegger, letter to Jean Beaufret of 23 November 1945, in *Basic Writings*, 2nd rev. edn, ed. D. F. Krell (New York: HarperCollins, 1993), p. 265.
16. René Char, 'A une sérénité crispée' ("A Tense Serenity") in his collected works (Paris: Gallimard, Pléiade, 1983), p. 753.

Note on The Bibliography

1. René Char, 'Feuillets d'Hypnos' ("The Leaves of Hypnos"), in his collected works (Paris: Gallimard, Pléiader, 1983), p. 190.
2. *Ibid.*, 'Les Matinaux' ("The Matinals"), p. 335.

Appendix: Chrono-Logies

1. A paper read at the time of the 'defence' of the doctoral thesis at the University of Louvain (Belgium) on 19 June 1993 before a jury presided over by M. Troisfontaines, president of the Institut Supérieur de Philosophie, and composed of MM. Derrida, Gérard, Ricoeur and Taminiaux ('promoter' of the thesis).
2. No. 26 of the series 'Philosophies' (Paris: P.U.F., 1990).
3. Dastur, *Hölderlin. Tragédie et modernité*, ("Hölderlin. Tragedy and Modernity") (Fougères: Encre Marine, 1992).
4. See the Prefatory Remarks of the editor, in this case Martin Heidegger, to the 'Vorlesungen zur Phänomenologie des inneren Zeitbewusstseins' ("Lectures on the Phenomenology of the Consciousness of Internal Time"), *Jahrbuch für Philosophie und phänomenologische Forschung IX* (Halle: Max Niemeyer, 1928).
5. See note 59 to *The Essence of Reasons*, trans. Terrence Malick (Evanston, IL: Northwestern University Press, 1969).

6. Cf. Heidegger, *What is Called Thinking?*, trans. J. Glenn Gray (New York: Harper and Row, 1968), p. 76: 'What is unthought in a thinker's thought is not a lack inherent in his thought. What is *un*-thought is there in each case only as the un-*thought*. The more original the thinker, the richer will be what is unthought in it. The unthought is the greatest gift a thought can bestow.'
7. Cf. *Sein und Zeit* (Tübingen: Niemeyer, 1953), p. 22 ff. English-language trans., *Being and Time*, trans. J. Stambaugh (Albany, NY: SUNY Press, 1996).
8. Cf. M. Merleau-Ponty, 'Philosophie et non philosophie depuis Hegel' (1), lecture notes, edited and introduced by Claude Lefort, in *Textures*, 8–9, 1974, p. 88; English-language trans., 'Philosophy and Non-Philosophy since Hegel', trans. Hugh J. Silverman, in *Philosophy and Non-Philosophy since Merleau-Ponty* (Evanston, IL: Northwestern University Press, 1988), p. 9.

Index

ATHLONE CONTEMPORARY EUROPEAN THINKERS

Aesthetic Theory
Adorno
0 485 30069 9 HB
0 485 30090 7 PB

Composing for the Films
Adorno & Eisler
0 485 11454 2 HB
0 485 12017 7 PB

Freud and Nietzsche
Assoun
0 485 11483 6 HB

Criticism and Truth
Barthes
0 485 12144 1 PB

Sollers Writer
Barthes
0 485 11337 6 PB

On Nietzsche
Bataille
0 485 30068 0 HB

Nietzsche: The Body and Culture
Blondel
0 485 11391 0 HB

Death: An Essay on Finitude
Dastur
0 485 11487 9 HB

Telling Time: Sketch of a Phenomenological Chronology
Dastur
0 485 11520 4 HB

Proust and Signs
Deleuze
0 485 12141 7 PB

Kant's Critical Philosophy
Deleuze
0 485 12101 8 PB

Difference and Repetition
Deleuze
0 485 11360 0 HB
0 485 12102 6 PB

The Fold: Leibniz and the Baroque
Deleuze
0 485 11421 6 HB
0 485 12087 9 PB

Anti-Oedipus: Capitalism and Schizophrenia
Deleuze & Guattari
Preface by Michel Foucault
0 485 30018 4 PB

A Thousand Plateaus
Deleuze & Guattari
0 485 11335 X HB
0 485 12058 4 PB

Cinema 1: The Movement-Image
Deleuze
0 485 12081 X PB

Cinema 2: The Time-Image
Deleuze
0 485 11359 7 HB
0 485 12070 4 PB

Dialogues
Deleuze & Parnet
0 485 11333 3 HB

Foucault
Deleuze
0 485 12154 9 PB

Logic of Sense
Deleuze
0 485 30063 X HB

Nietzsche and Philosophy
Deleuze
0 485 12053 4 PB

Dissemination
Derrida
0 485 12093 3 PB

Positions
Derrida
0 485 30000 1 HB
0 485 12055 0 PB

The Memory of Thought: On Heidegger and Adorno
Düttmann
0 485 11489 5 HB

The Gift of Language: Memory and Promise in Adorno, Benjamin, Heidegger and Rosenzweig
Düttmann
0 485 11488 7 HB

Nietzsche's Philosophy
Fink
0 485 11484 4 HB

Death and the Labyrinth: The World of Raymond Roussel
Foucault
0 485 11336 8 HB
0 485 12059 3 PB

Three Ecologies
Guattari
0 485 11555 7 HB

pleroma – Reading in Hegel
Hamacher
0 485 11457 7 HB

Towards the Definition of Philosophy
Heidegger
0 485 11508 5 HB

The Nature of Truth
Heidegger
0 485 11509 3 HB

On the Essence of Human Freedom
Heidegger
0 485 11516 6 HB

Phenomenology of Intuition and Expression
Heidegger
0 485 11415 8 HB

Speech is Never Neuter
Irigaray
0 485 11452 9 HB
0 485 12089 5 PB

Democracy Between Two
Irigaray
0 485 11503 4 HB
0 485 12123 9 PB

To Be Two
Irigaray
0 485 11492 5 HB
0 485 12120 4 PB

The Forgetting of Air
Irigaray
0 485 11491 7 HB
0 485 12119 0 PB

Elemental Passions
Irigaray
0 485 11409 7 HB
0 485 12079 8 PB

An Ethics of Sexual Difference
Irigaray
0 485 30067 2 HB
0 485 30070 2 PB

Nietzsche and the Vicious Circle
Klossowski
0 485 11440 2 HB

Explosion I
Kofman
0 485 11458 5 HB

Explosion II
Kofman
0 485 11459 3 HB

Camera Obscura: of Ideology
Kofman
0 485 11490 9 HB

Socrates: Fictions of a Philospher
Kofman
0 485 11460 7 HB

Nietzsche and Metaphor
Kofman
0 485 11422 4 HB
0 485 12098 4 PB

The Philosophical Imaginary
Le Doeuff
0 485 11352 X HB

Alterity & Transcendence
Levinas
0 485 11519 0 HB
0 485 12152 2 PB

Entre Nous: Essays on Thinking-of-the-Other
Levinas
0 485 11465 8 HB

Proper Names
Levinas
0 485 11466 6 HB

In the Time of the Nations
Levinas
0 485 11449 6 HB

Beyond the Verse
Levinas
0 485 11430 5 HB

Outside the Subject
Levinas
0 485 11412 7 HB
0 485 12097 6 PB

Difficult Freedom: Essays on Judaism
Levinas
0 485 11379 1 HB

Redemption and Utopia
Löwy
0 485 11406 2 HB

Sex and Existence: Simone de Beauvoir's The Second Sex
Lundgren-Gothlin
Preface by Toril Moi
0 485 11469 0 HB
0 485 12124 7 PB

Libidinal Economy
Lyotard
0 485 12083 6 PB

The Conflict of Interpretations: Essays in Hermeneutics I
Ricoeur
0 485 30061 3 HB

From Text to Action: Essays in Hermeneutics II
Ricouer
0 485 30064 8 PB

Hegel: Contra Sociology
Rose
0 485 12036 4 PB

Clavis Universalis
Rossi
0 485 11468 2 HB

Friedrich Nietzsche: An Introduction
Vattimo
0 485 11485 2 HB
0 485 12118 2 PB